Shepherd Leadership

The Metrics that Really Matter

CRAIG T. OWENS

FREILING
PUBLISHING

Published by Freiling Publishing, a division of Freiling Agency, LLC.

P.O. Box 1264
Warrenton, VA 20188

www.FreilingPublishing.com

ISBN: 978-1-950948-98-7

Printed in the United States of America

DEDICATION

For those who believed in me before I even believed
in myself: my parents, my wife, my family, my covenant
brother, my church.

TABLE OF CONTENTS

FOREWORD

I learned to drive in Africa where cows, goats, sheep, and camels often graze on the shoulders of narrow roads. From far away you can tell the difference between a sheep and a goat—the tail of the goat turns up, and the tail of the sheep down. This is important because goats are smart and turn away from traffic while dumb sheep waltz out in front of speeding death.

We all, like dumb sheep, have turned away from safety and sauntered out in front of speeding death (Isaiah 53:6). Stunningly, the Good Shepherd has put the care of His foolish flock into the hands of under-shepherds who tend to be somewhat stupid ourselves. The grand gamble only works if under-shepherds studiously lead in the way that Jesus instructed us to—and therein is the rub, for none of us naturally agrees with His model. Our flesh, culture, ambitions, and propensities all fight Shepherd Leadership like the plague. We may kiss the concept theoretically, but we fundamentally flee from it functionally.

We don't mind serving Jesus, for we know we are naturally inferior to Him. We don't even mind serving little lambs, for we perceive ourselves as superior to them. Where our struggle is exposed is in serving fellow sheep. Yet Jesus donned a towel and lifted dirty feet (John 13:14), giving us the example to wash one another's feet. We make much of Jesus by being little in our own eyes, and there is no better test of this than in how we think of ourselves in comparison to our peers.

As under-shepherds, we cloak our drive for superiority well. We have conflated task with title and have made nickels and noses the measure of success. We conveniently forget that Jesus asked, "What man of you will not leave the ninety-nine?" (John 15:4). We ignore the reminder that we must give away all to be His disciples (Luke 14:33).

But what if Jesus is right? What if the best leaders are actually sheep who serve other sheep in hidden and uncelebrated ways? What if the best leaders are the unknown ones, the ones without a lot of lambs or dollars, the ones who daily lay down their sheep lives for other sheep? I have a sneaking feeling that those 24 elders around the throne will be those who best served fellow sheep.

God plucked David from the sheepfold. God chose a sheep to be a shepherd. And though we all are stupid sheep, when God plucks us out of obscurity to serve others, we can have the humble confidence for as long as we are asked to lead that God has chosen us. That confidence both faithfully drives us to our knees and fearlessly propels us against our giants. It is good to be a sheep; it is good to be an under-shepherd. Just remember you are stupid, chosen by the Wise One, and as long as you serve as a shepherd, you and your flock will be safe.

The book you are about to read is a refreshing look at leading as a sheep, of serving like our Chief Shepherd. I trust you will benefit from it as much as I did.

Dr. Dick Brogden. Jr.
Co-founder of the Live Dead Movement
Saudi Arabia, June 2021

PREFACE

I have set you an example. —*Jesus Christ*

Chris, a colleague who worked with me at our after-school youth center, walked in one afternoon and greeted me with a rather odd question: "Craig, do you prefer to be called the 'lead pastor' or the 'senior pastor'?"

I smiled and said, "That's a rather weird question to start the afternoon!"

Chris explained, "We were just working on a new organizational flowchart at our church, and there was quite a lengthy discussion on what the title for our pastor should be. I heard lots of pros and cons on the two different titles, and I was just wondering what your take is."

I silently continued to smile at Chris until he finally smiled back and said, "I know. You're going to say, 'Which title is in the Bible?'"

Bingo!

I'm not going to get on my soapbox here and rail on titles or flowcharts, because actually I somewhat enjoy those organizational tools. I have frequently been asked to come into floundering organizations as a consultant, and very quickly I'm able to assess some areas of inefficiency and suggest some operational changes that can help put them back on track. And I really have no problem with titles *per se*. I do, however, have a problem with spending too much valuable time on finding the right title to fill in our carefully designed organizational charts. This is creative energy that could be spent much more profitably somewhere else.

My larger concern is that churches, parachurch organizations, and nonprofit ministries that are largely founded to fulfill a biblical mandate are straying from the simple, freeing truths found in the Bible. Or maybe I should say that they are adding things to their ministries that aren't in the pages of Scripture. Whichever way you want to say it, the result is the same: We are using the wrong metrics to define "success" for our ministries. I fear that in our focus on unbiblical practices, we are missing the joy of really doing ministry.

All of these titles, flowcharts, and non-essential things that we are discussing, revamping, implementing, and measuring aren't doing anything to liberate us, but they are keeping us focused on checking off meaningless boxes. We're spending far too much valuable time and resources on keeping the machinery running, but we're not correctly evaluating the outputs. We need to recalibrate our understanding of leadership: God's leaders are servants.

What does this serving leader look like? I believe the best picture is found in Christ's own words: "I am the Good Shepherd." Throughout the Bible, God frequently refers to those in leadership positions as shepherds. I like the idea of leaders as shepherds.

Shepherds don't try to get their sheep to move through an organizational flowchart, they don't care what title the sheep give them, and they aren't looking for applause from the sheep for a job well done. Shepherds are just looking for the best way to care for their sheep—to get them the nutrition they need, to protect them from dangers, and to place them where they can be healthy. Only healthy sheep reproduce healthy sheep. Shepherds don't reproduce sheep, but they simply foster the environment where the sheep can be at their optimum health.

I believe that leaders of churches and nonprofit ministries will find the greatest freedom and enjoyment—and ultimately experience the full blessing of God—when they learn to view themselves as shepherd leaders. Jesus is our ultimate example: Our Good Shepherd showed us how to live out the lifestyle that pleases Him and glorifies our Heavenly Father.

My prayer is that this book liberates you! I want to see all of us get back to the simple shepherding style of leadership that the Bible has portrayed for us, so that our ministries are healthy, energized, effective, sheep-producing, and God-glorifying.

1

THE WRONG LADDER

He that is down needs fear no fall.
—John Bunyan

"What's your growth plan?" the older, and presumably wiser, mentor asked.

The young man looked a bit confused. "My growth plan?"

"Yes," the older man asked, "what are you prepared to do so that you can climb the ladder?" Before the younger man could answer, this passionate older leader began to explain about "paying your dues" and "putting in your time" and "meeting the right people," all so that advancement possibilities were still in play. "In other words," he concluded, "what's your plan to be successful?"

Maybe you've been a part of a conversation like this, either as the one talking to a young person, or on the receiving end.

Or maybe, like many people, you've been working on a plan to climb your own ladder of success. You've been careful to get the best education, meet the right people, and put in the right amount of time on each level, all while keeping your eyes and ears open for the next "rung" of the ladder.

Perhaps this is successful in the corporate world, but I wonder how this idea has crept into the ministry world. Make no mistake: this mindset is prominent in our churches and nonprofit organizations. We may dress it up in churchy language, but the attitude is still there.

We may counsel a young person to go to the right Bible college and to find a good church to start as a youth pastor and maybe move up to an associate pastor. Eventually, after putting in the necessary time and paying his dues, he can become the pastor of a small church or a small nonprofit organization. If the leader does well in that small organization—proven by increasing the number of attendees and donors—he can then move into a larger organization. After showing success for a number of years—again, "success" being defined as more people and more money—the minister might become an author or a consultant until he finally retires and lives out the remainder of his days on his well-earned retirement funds.

Does that sound familiar? It may sound familiar to our modern-day ears, but nowhere in the pages of Scripture is such a corporate ladder ever portrayed for us.

God's Measure of Success

God frequently picks people we would consider the least qualified. He sometimes has one in an unglamorous position for years, and sometimes He catapults some-body immediately to the top. Sometimes God will keep His hand-selected individual in a prominent leadership position until death, and sometimes He will remove that person to a place of obscurity after only a short time.

God's ladder of success is nothing like ours!

There are some tricky problems for us when we attempt to run God-honoring ministries in ways that God never designed. First, and most obvious, we are arrogantly asking for God's blessing on something He cannot bless. We are saying to Him, "God, this is *my* plan; please bless it." Instead, we should be saying, "God, show me *Your* plan because I want to do what You are blessing."

Second, we set ourselves up for disappointment. If we are gauging success by how high and fast we climb some ladder of success that we've designed, or if we are basing our effectiveness on how many people or donors we've generated, we are bound to be disappointed. Take, for example, a pandemic or an economic turndown that constricts nearly everything. Since our numbers have decreased, does that mean we've failed? As John Bunyan reminded us, a servant who is already kneeling down to serve has no fear of falling.

Probably the most dangerous consequence is that we can begin to treat people as a means to an end—that end being "my success." After all, if the ladder we're climbing is determined by bigger numbers, then we'll do whatever it takes just to get the numbers to increase. In so doing, we lose sight that ministry is about *people*, not about *numbers*.

In John 13, Jesus prepared to share a final meal with His disciples. John recorded these words: "Jesus knew that God had put all things under His power" (v. 3). **ALL things**—not some limited power, but *all* power. At that moment, Jesus was, without question, the most powerful Person standing on planet earth. By modern-day standards, we could say Jesus had reached the top of the ladder!

What would you do with that much power? How would you respond to having God's full approval?

Here's what Jesus did: He took on the role of the lowest of servants and washed His disciples' feet. Then after doing this, He said something He had never said to His disciples before: "I have set you an example that you should do as I have done for you" (v. 14).

Jesus used His unlimited power to serve.

Our Good Shepherd's plan all along was to serve people. He said, "The Son of Man did not come to be served, but to serve and to give His life as a ransom for many" (Mark 10:45).

Quite simply stated: Shepherd leaders serve.

Or let me say it another way: God-honoring shepherd leaders embody servanthood. Serving is not just something shepherd leaders do, but it is also who they are, how they think, how they plan, and how they measure success. We've mistakenly flipped the example that Jesus gave us: we've been trying to climb up while Jesus has given us the example to kneel down.

At that same supper where Jesus washed His disciples' feet and told them that this was the example for them to follow, the disciples had an argument among themselves about the pecking order. They were trying to figure out where they stood on the organizational flowchart. Once again, Jesus tried to redirect them to His example:

> Jesus told them, "In this world the kings and great men lord it over their people, yet they are called 'friends of the people.'" **But among you it will be different.** Those who are the greatest among you should take the lowest rank, and **the leader should be like a servant.** Who is more important, the one who sits at the table or the one who serves? The one who sits at the table, of course. But

not here! **For I am among you as one who serves.**
(Luke 22:25–27 NLT, emphasis mine)

The shepherd leader isn't attempting to chart his own path to success, but he is growing in his understanding that success is finding more ways to serve. The shepherd leader isn't looking to advance himself, but he is watching and listening for more opportunities to serve. The shepherd leader understands that advancement comes only in God's timing, and that any position of leadership is only a temporary position of servitude.

If we truly want to be considered successful, we must turn our backs on what is typically termed "success" so that we can keep our eyes on our Chief Shepherd. See the One with all power using His unlimited power to stoop down to serve. That's the posture servant-hearted shepherds continually aspire to take, and that's the posture that God wholeheartedly approves.

2

SECURE TO SERVE

I believe there is no one Principle, which predominates
in human Nature so much in every stage of Life ...
as this Passion for Superiority.
—*John Adams*

I was wrestling some empty cardboard boxes, attempting to get them to lie flat so I could get them into the recycling dumpster, when I was interrupted by a voice behind me.

"Excuse me," she said through her open car window.

"How can I help you?" I asked as I gladly took a break from the unwieldy cardboard.

"I'm wondering where I can unload all of my supplies for our conference this weekend."

"How about right here?" I offered with a smile. "Just pull up next to the curb, and we can go in through this door."

She pulled over and popped the car trunk open. I took a look at the stack of books, folders for her attendees, and all of her presentation materials to assess what I would need to help her. "If you'll come with me, I'll show you to your conference room."

"What about all of my things?" she wondered.

"I'll take care of it for you," I smiled. "And if you're comfortable letting me drive your car, I'll even park it for you when I'm done."

After escorting her to the conference room where she would be conducting her women's retreat for the weekend, I made several trips to and from her car to deliver all of her materials. After parking her car, I brought one of our guest services directors with me so that our guest could finalize all of her weekend details.

Just before dinnertime, I was finishing up some things in my office. My office was at the end of the hallway where nearly everyone coming or going to our dining facility would pass by. As a rule, I routinely left my office door open so I could be readily accessible if my team needed me.

As the lady I had previously helped was on her way to dinner with a large group of her conference attendees, she sort of half-turned to glance in my office door as she was walking by. Then she stopped dead in her tracks so suddenly that she nearly caused the women behind her to tumble over her. She looked at the sign on my door that said "Director," and then she looked at me behind my desk. She looked at the sign again, and then looked at me again. I smiled, stood up from behind my desk, and began to walk toward her. "Is there anything else I can do for you?" I offered.

She stepped into my office with a curious look on her face. "You're the conference center director," she said, half as a statement and half as a question.

"That's what they tell me," I laughed.

"But... but...," she stammered, "You carried in all of my materials, and you parked my car, and you were breaking down boxes, and..." she trailed off. I just smiled at her, trying to process what was going through her mind. "And... and... you're *the director!*"

"Yep," I said, "and I'm so happy to have been available to do all of those things for you."

The Serving Attitude

Why did this so surprise our guest? I think it's because we have developed a series of tasks that are "beneath" certain titles. We, quite wrongly, think that certain levels on the organizational chart exempt us from certain tasks that are only for those on the lower levels.

But this was certainly not the mindset of Jesus. Remember in John 13 we saw that Jesus was the most powerful person on the planet, and that He used all of this authority to step into the lowest of low roles: a washer of dirty feet. Actually, I think it was precisely because He knew how powerful He was that He was empowered to serve.

Only secure people can serve. Insecure people think that by serving, people will look down on them or take advantage of them. Only people who are absolutely certain that they are doing exactly what God has called them to do have no fear of "losing their place." If my mindset is that success is measured by how far I've climbed up the ladder, how many people report to me, how big my organization's budget is, or what tasks I no longer need to do because they are now beneath me, then anything that might jeopardize that position of status is to be avoided at all costs. Insecure leaders won't do things they perceive to be on a "lower level" because they think they might be reassigned to that level and lose some of their prestige.

Jesus—invested with all power—said, "I am among you **as one who serves**" (Luke 22:27). What would make us think that we can do anything else?

We have to get to a place where we are secure in the position God has placed us, always remembering that since He placed us, He is the only one who can remove us. There is, of course, a double-edged sword in this confidence in our calling. If confidence is not tempered by humility, we can easily become brash, conceited, and ultimately disqualified for the position.

I am forever grateful for the insights of two men who helped me get a handle on this duality of a shepherd leader's confident humility (or if you prefer, humble confidence). J. Oswald Sanders in his book *Spiritual Leadership* and Kenneth Blanchard in his book *Lead Like Jesus* have given us a healthy model.

There is nothing wrong about aspiring to a leadership position. The apostle Paul wrote to his young protégé Timothy, "This is a trustworthy saying: 'If someone aspires to be a church leader, he desires an honorable position'" (1 Timothy 3:1 NLT). Yet this desire needs to be tempered by Jeremiah's words to his scribe Baruch, "Should you then seek great things for yourself? Do not seek them" (Jeremiah 45:5). Taken together, a shepherd leader's passion for greater leadership should be to gain greater things not for himself but for others.

Shepherd leaders need to remind themselves frequently of this simple statement: God chose me. The confidence comes from remembering "God chose." If God has chosen me, then He has also equipped me. He foresaw the needs of this organization, and He has prepared me to step into this role for such a time as this. The humility comes from remembering "God chose *me*." Who am I that God would think so highly of me? Of all the people on Earth that God could have placed here, why did He pick me? This confident humility will do two things for us: keep us confident to continue to lead when doubts or naysayers arise, and keep us humble to continue to serve people when pride or applause arises.

A great biblical example is a man who was key in the early growth of the New Testament church, a Levite named Joseph. As a Levite, Joseph was born into a family line that carried a certain amount of prestige. He had a secure future following the millennia of worship leaders who had come before him. Talk about security!

Yet Joseph somehow came to know about Jesus, believing Him to be the promised Messiah. Joseph was willing to give up everything that held him secure, even selling family property to give the proceeds to the newly formed Church. He became such an encourager to the Christians that they give him the nickname Barnabas, which was an exalted title meaning "son of a prophet." Later on, some Greeks in Lystra were so enamored with the powerful ministry of Joseph Barnabas that they called him Zeus, the chief of the Greek gods. Barnabas could have leveraged these titles to give himself a very secure position in the Church that no one would have questioned.

Another meaning of the name Barnabas can be "the encourager." This man never sought the limelight, but he was constantly seeking ways to serve others. He used this confidence of God's calling to humbly serve. Not only did he give up his property to supply much needed funds to the

Church, but he was also the first one to see the potential in a new Christian convert named Saul. When the rest of the Church looked at Saul suspiciously, Barnabas mentored him, introduced him to the other Church leaders, and gave Saul/Paul his first leadership role.

We see the humble side of Barnabas' confident humility in the way he allowed Paul to surpass him and take the lead in their missionary journey. It's interesting to note how specific the historian Luke was in all of his records. Luke listed the names of people in order of their prominence. As the first missionary journey commenced, Barnabas was listed first, but as the journey proceeded, Paul moved into the "first chair" as Barnabas stepped back. Even after Paul and Barnabas had a disagreement over whether or not Mark should be given another place on their team, it was Barnabas who willingly gave up co-leadership of the next missionary trip so he could keep Mark with him while he mentored him to greater maturity. Later on, Mark was referred to in glowing terms by two key Church leaders: Paul and Peter (2 Timothy 4:11; 1 Peter 5:13).

What a great example of a shepherd leader! Barnabas was secure enough to lead boldly and humble enough to serve without recognition. His confident humility or humble confidence allowed him to move easily between roles without ever feeling slighted.

Here are two great questions for every shepherd leader to ponder to make sure that we are remaining both secure and humble in our calling:

Q: How do I know if I am a servant?

A: If people treat me like a servant.

Q: How do I know if I have a God-honoring servant's attitude?

A: If I don't mind it when people treat me like a servant.

God wants to use you as a leader. He has called you to great things. Just remember that He does the calling and the equipping *so that* you can serve and shepherd others. It may be a prominent, noticeable position, or it may be an obscure position unseen by very many. It may be a position God keeps you in until the day He calls you home, or it may be a temporary position. A humbly confident leader doesn't fight to climb a ladder nor strive to keep a position on a higher rung of the ladder. The shepherd leader is confident to serve where God places him, and humble enough to be moved, or even removed, as God sees best. But most of all, a secure shepherd leader knows that God's desire for His leader in any position is a heart to serve others.

3

SHEPHERD LEADERSHIP

True shepherds go to their sheep,
where they are, to watch over their souls
and equip them for ministry.
—*T.M. Moore*

It's humorous to watch how traditions and even vocabulary get passed along from generation to generation without anyone questioning why. I'm sure you've heard or experienced numerous examples of someone doing or saying something just because "it's always been done or said that way."

In overseeing an after-school youth center, I have worked with middle-school students for over a decade. Every year brings in a new crop of fresh-faced sixth graders and sees the "graduation" of our students who are heading off to high school. I love hanging out with these young people every afternoon!

Our program meets in one of the buildings on our public school campus, so I patterned many of our rules and procedures directly from the school's student handbook. I observed that the students all referred to their teachers in a traditional way, which is also somewhat formal, such as Mr. Smith, Mrs. Jones, or Miss White. I wanted to continue this pattern of respect, but since we were meeting after school was dismissed, I also wanted to lighten it up just a bit.

So in my very first year as the director of this program, I introduced myself to the students as "Pastor Craig." I thought this kept a title that the students were used to using throughout their school day, but also made it a little less formal than "Pastor Owens." Any of our youth pastors that were working as staff with me I introduced the same way—Pastor Joe, Pastor Josh, Pastor Chris, and so on. Much to my surprise, the youth pastors were addressed by the students just as I had introduced them, but for me, I was quickly called merely "Pastor."

As my second year working with our students began, there were so many returning students who already knew all of our staff members, I didn't even think about doing introductions on the first day of the new school year. After all, the students were already addressing our youth pastors as "Pastor Josh" and calling me simply "Pastor."

A favorite activity each afternoon is a game of foosball against me. The students can have the traditional two-person team, but I play by myself. I offer the prize of free food for the winners. To make things a bit more sporting, I spot the students a few goals before we even start. Students stand in line for a chance to play me—especially on pizza days—to try to win the coveted food (and perhaps some bragging rights, too).

One day, in the middle of a very competitive game, I was engaging in a little friendly trash-talking, trying to distract my young opponents a bit. One of the sixth-grade students laughed and said, "Nice try, Pasture, but you can't distract me!"

His teammate stopped mid-play and looked at his friend with wide open eyes. "Pasture?! Did you just call him 'Pasture'?"

The sixth grader innocently replied, "Uh, yeah. What's the big deal?"

The older (and much wiser) student informed him, "He's not a cow! We're not putting him out in the *pasture!*"

This young sixth grader had heard all of the students calling me "Pastor," but having no frame of reference for what they were actually saying, he misheard it as "Pasture." We all had a good laugh and resumed our game (which I won, by the way).

We all still smile about this innocent misunder-standing, although several of my staff members still delight in calling me *"Pasture* Craig" every now and then. I had a conversation with this sixth grader later on. I found out he had never been to church and therefore didn't know that a pastor would be someone who oversees the activities of a church. He was simply mimicking a title that he thought others were using.

Allow me to contrast this lighthearted moment with a more serious exchange in which the lack of a title was almost someone's undoing.

I was once working with a larger organization, where the leader was a bit of an old-school, top-down leader. Everything was done in a very formal way, including the way he was to be addressed as "Pastor Smith" (this is not his actual name). Everyone on staff and all of the stake-holders in this organization called him this, even at times his own wife.

A new staff member named Jim (also not his actual name) had just joined us, and on his first day he was unpacking some things in his office as I was standing in his doorway going over a few policies and procedures. While we were talking, Pastor Smith entered the main office, picked up his telephone messages, and began to walk down the hallway toward his own office.

"Excuse me," said Jim, as he pushed his way past me in the doorway and stepped out into the hallway. "Hey, Bill!" he yelled down the hallway to Pastor Smith.

You could have heard a pin drop in the office! Pastor Smith stopped dead in his tracks, and all of the staff members seemed frozen in place wondering what was going to happen. Just like at the youth center where I didn't think to introduce myself at the start of the second year, I never thought to tell Jim the proper use of titles around this place.

Jim immediately sensed that he done something wrong, although he couldn't figure it out at first. Pastor Smith called me into his office a few minutes later and instructed me to explain to Jim the proper etiquette among the staff. It was only as I shared this with Jim that it dawned on him the huge mistake he had made. Unlike the chuckle my youth center staff got out of my new title of "Pasture" Craig, none of this organization's office staff laughed about Jim's faux pas. Actually, everyone felt bad for his rough first-day experience.

What's in a Title?

People who are carefully tracking their climb up their organization's flowchart love their titles! It's a badge of success and an ongoing mark of authority. Heaven help you if you use the wrong title or fail to use any title at all.

But I've found that leaders who are confidently humble in the roles in which God has called them couldn't care less what title someone may or may not use.

Let's consider the title of "pastor." Where did this come from in the first place? In the New Testament church, we see roles of apostle, prophet, evangelist, elder, teacher, and overseer. But please note that these are always *roles* and not titles. No one addresses Paul as "Apostle Paul." In a personal letter, Paul tells Timothy to do the work of an evangelist, but he doesn't refer to Timothy as "Evangelist Timothy" in his other letters. Somewhere along the line, we've made the task we are doing to be the title, and the title to be a mark of achievement to show where we are on the flowchart. Then, as I related earlier, we spend far too much precious time figuring out what specific title each one in our organization should have.

In actuality, my sixth-grade friend was closer to the truth than he ever will know. When Paul lists the gifts that Jesus gave to the church, he says, "It was [Jesus] who gave some to be apostles, some to be prophets, some to be evangelists, and some to be pastors and teachers" (Ephesians 4:11). The Greek word Paul chose for pastors is *poimēn* which, prior to being used in a church setting, meant "one who tends flocks or herds; a shepherd."

I believe Paul may have chosen this word because God Himself used a similar word in the Old Testament to talk about those who were supposed to be taking care of His flock of people (see Jeremiah 2:8; 3:15; 10:21; 12:10; 17:16). It's the same title God uses for Himself (Isaiah 40:11), for rulers who are doing His bidding (Isaiah 44:28), and for those who literally care for sheep and herds (Jeremiah 25:35; Luke 2:8). And most telling of all, it's also the term used for Jesus (John 10:11–16; Hebrews 13:20).

All church leaders have been given a charge from God to lead people, but God didn't give anyone a title. We are the ones that have turned a calling into a title, and the title into a mark of authority.

Leaders as Shepherds

I really like the idea of leaders as shepherds, because shepherds have to take care of some pretty unwieldy animals that clearly don't care about titles or flowcharts. Sheep can be loving animals, but they require an immense amount of care from someone who is intimately aware of each sheep's temperament and needs. Sheep cannot be cared for in a cookie-cutter, mass-produced, assembly-line-style program.

Easton's Bible Dictionary quotes a passage from William Deane's book *David* that is a good overview of the challenges of shepherding:

In early morning [the shepherd] led forth the flock from the fold, marching at its head to the spot where they were to be pastured. Here he watched them all day, taking care that none of the sheep strayed, and if any for a time eluded his watch and wandered away from the rest, seeking diligently till he found and brought it back. In those lands sheep require to be supplied regularly with water, and the shepherd for this purpose has to guide them either to some running stream or to wells dug in the wilderness and furnished with troughs. At night he brought the flock home to the fold, counting them as they passed under the rod at the door to assure himself that none were missing. Nor did his labours always end with sunset. Often he had to guard the fold through the dark hours from the attack of wild beasts, or the wily attempts of the prowling thief (see 1 Samuel 17:34).

Can you hear the echoes of my sixth-grade friend in Deane's phrase about leading the sheep "to the spot where they were to be *pastured*"? How accurate he was in his innocent misstatement!

David was the most powerful leader Israel ever had, and he is lauded for leading God's people with integrity and skill like a shepherd. Not as a warlord, not as a kingdom builder, not as a musician and songwriter; but a lowly, unassuming shepherd.

I like this description from *The Amplified Bible*:

> *[God] chose David His servant and took him from the sheepfolds; from tending the ewes that had their young He brought him to be the shepherd of Jacob His people, of Israel His inheritance. So David was their shepherd with an upright heart; he guided them by the discernment and skillfulness which controlled his hands.* (Psalm 78:70–72)

Notice that God chose David precisely because of his servant's heart (1 Samuel 13:14). David was pasturing his sheep when Samuel called him in to anoint him as king of Israel, and David immediately returned to caring for his sheep after being anointed (1 Samuel 16:11–13; 17:15). God saw a shepherd with a heart full of love for Himself and for other people, and He said, "This man will go from caring for his father's sheep to caring for My sheep."

God didn't give David a title but a position of responsibility. David carried out his new position with the same loving care that he had done with his sheep. When Psalm 78:72 says, "David was their shepherd," the Hebrew word means "one who pastures": He pastured God's people with integrity and with skill.

David exhibited the leadership qualities that shepherds are known for. Notice the similarities between a good shepherd and *the* Good Shepherd Jesus:

1. Shepherds don't see their sheep as a mass, but they know each and every individual sheep by name. Jesus said He knew His sheep and His sheep knew Him (John 10:4, 14).

2. Shepherds lead their flock by walking in the middle of the group so that they can be as close to as many sheep as possible. Jesus said He "leads them out" and walks among them (John 10:4).

3. Shepherds are attentive to the particular needs of the young, the sick, and the elderly. Just as David was gently and attentively "following the ewes that had young," Jesus came as a physician for the sick (Luke 5:31).

4. Shepherds lie down in the dirt to protect any places vulnerable to a predator's attack. Jesus was the door to the sheepfold and the protector of the sheep (John 10:7, 15).

5. Shepherds find the best food and water possible for their sheep. Jesus became the living bread and the living water for His people (John 6:35; 4:13–14).

6. Shepherds search for any sheep that have strayed. Jesus is always on a rescue mission for wayward sheep (John 10:16; Luke 15:3-7).

The bottom line: David shepherded the people of Israel just as he himself had been shepherded by God.

These are still the types of people God wants to use as His shepherd leaders today: Those who will pasture people in a confidently humble manner, those who are not hung up on titles, and those who are not looking for an easy assignment.

Those people who want the title and the authority, but not the grind and messiness and challenges of pasturing sheep, Jesus calls them out as mere hirelings at best, and robbers and thieves at worst.

Shepherds never get many accolades while they are leading sheep. In fact, sheep tend to bite and stray more often than they applaud. But those shepherd leaders who have a heart for God, who are confident that God called them, and who are humble enough to get down in the dirt with the sheep, those are the leaders God loves to reward.

4

A CONFIDENT LEADER'S ATTITUDE ADJUSTMENT

An attitude of submission is not a loss of authority.
It is a recognition of the source of authority.
—*Mike Bonem and Roger Patterson*

I once attended a basketball game where the halftime entertainment included a woman named Red Panda on an extraordinarily tall unicycle. As if keeping that unicycle balanced while she zipped around the basketball court wasn't enough, she began placing bowls on one foot and flipping them up into the air, only to catch and balance them on her head! The stack of bowls continued to grow and grow, all while she kept both the stack balanced on her head and herself balanced on her unicycle. It was quite impressive!

Every leader has a similar balancing act. God has created each of us uniquely—implanted with the temperament, talents, and personality He wanted each of us to have. God made you on purpose, and He made you for a purpose. But that being said, shepherd leaders are almost never perfectly balanced. If you've ever taken a temperaments assessment or any other kind of personality test, you know that you had some attributes that were more prominent than others. God never gives us weaknesses, but our areas of strength can become a self-imposed weakness if we rely on our strength instead of on our Strength Giver.

Leaders tend toward two poles: confidence or humility. God made us this way on purpose. But to be the best shepherd leader, we each must allow the Holy Spirit to help us learn to lead in a more balanced way. If we lean too much toward confidence, we can come across as arrogant and even tyrannical. But if we lean too much toward humility, we can appear to be weak, indecisive, and unsure of our leadership direction. None of us will be perfect in this at every single moment, but with the proper attitude adjustments, we can learn to more consistently stay at the balanced point of being humbly confident or confidently humble.

If God designed you to be naturally confident, you will have no problem charging ahead toward the goal of moving the flock under your care by the sheer force of your will. You will get the organization moving, but you may injure sheep and end up leaving several sheep behind as you aggressively grow the organization.

On the other hand, if God wired you to be more humble, you can easily defer too much to others because you never want to step on anyone's toes. Sheep in your organization love you and they love each other. No one gets injured or left behind, but the organization itself doesn't seem to be producing the results that would keep it viable.

The confident will need to focus on humility, and the humble will need to focus on confidence. The Holy Spirit can help you find and maintain that sweet spot of humble confidence. As you mature as a shepherd leader, you will discover that you are increasingly successful at staying balanced between these two poles. John Maxwell noted, "Servanthood is not about position or skill. It's about attitude." And there is no better attitude adjuster than the Holy Spirit!

The first step in this adjustment process is self-awareness. A great place to start is with a prayer that the shepherd leader David gave us:

Search me, God, and know my heart; test me and know my anxious thoughts. See if there is any offensive way in me, and lead me in the way everlasting. (Psalm 139:23–24)

Shepherd leaders should make this a regular prayer. Pray it and listen closely as God will speak to your heart about areas that have become out of balance and therefore "offensive" and counterproductive to your leadership.

In this chapter, I want to address those leaders who tend naturally toward confidence. In the following chapter, we'll discuss those leaders who are naturally wired toward humility.

Dialing Back the Confidence

So let's talk about how the overly confident leader can add the correct dose of humility that will bring about the proper balance.

I really like how C.S. Lewis defines humility: "Humility isn't thinking less of yourself; it's thinking of yourself less."

When the focus is on me, it's hard—if not impossible—to be humble, but when the focus is on others, it's hard to be overly confident.

Humility is often misunderstood as allowing others to advance, and in so doing, I am completely overlooked. Others get the accolades and I get nothing. As a result, humility has gotten a bad reputation. People begin to think of a humble person as someone who never speaks up for himself, someone who can be taken advantage of, someone who becomes a doormat for everyone else. But the picture of a humble person in the Bible couldn't be more different!

We all have to bow to someone or something. The humble shepherd leader has chosen to bow to God and to follow God's righteous standards. One name for God is Jehovah Tsidkenu, which means God is righteous (see Psalm 119:137). The Hebrew word *tsadhe* is a part of God's righteous title, and it's how we are called to live. *Tsadhe* means the humble, faithful servant.

Jesus lists a whole series of rewards for those who are humbly and faithfully dependent on God for help in the Beatitudes (Matthew 5:3–12), concluding by saying, "Rejoice and be glad, because great is your reward in heaven!"

When you zoom in on the Hebrew letter *tsadhe*, you will see that the faithful, humble, kneeling servant is depicted with a crown. Far from being pushed down, left behind, or left unrewarded, the humble person is the one God delights to exalt!

Jesus made a deliberate choice to set aside all of His prerogatives as the Son of God by deliberately "making Himself nothing by taking the very nature of a servant" and purposefully continuing to "[humble] Himself by becoming obedient to death" (Philippians 2:7–8). Jesus was confident in who He was, so He was secure enough to serve even the lowliest servants. As He bowed in humility, He struck the perfect balance of humble confidence, which allowed God to crown Him and to "[exalt] Him to the highest place and [give] Him the name that is above every name" (v. 9).

Paul begins this description of Christ's humble confidence with these words for all shepherd leaders who would follow Christ's example: "Let this same attitude and purpose and humble mind be in you which was in Christ Jesus" (v. 5, Amplified Bible). If confidence is your natural temperament, you are going to have to deliberately instill this attitude in your heart. You will need to find a way to actively serve the servants.

Plunger Man!

Not to be too graphic or gross, but younger kids struggle in using bathroom facilities, especially when they are in a public restroom, Mom or Dad isn't around to coach them, and they are in a hurry to get back to the fun activities with their friends. This was on full display for my team when we would host upwards of 500 children for a week of summer camp fun.

My housekeeping staff didn't look forward to these weeks. We literally had to schedule teams to monitor and clean up dozens of restrooms all over the campground all day long. I'm not exaggerating here—it was truly an all-day operation. I knew they really dreaded getting this assignment. It wasn't necessarily something I relished either, but as one who by natural temperament is highly confident, I needed to make sure I beefed up my servant's attitude.

I had to make a deliberate choice to serve the servants—to do the work that no one else wanted to do, and to serve my staff by (if you'll pardon the pun) *relieving* them of at least a little of their distasteful work. So I created an alter-ego superhero named Plunger Man.

I'd go to bed at my usual time, but then I would get up in the middle of the night, slip on some work clothes, and begin making the rounds of all the restrooms. I wore rubber gloves nearly up to my elbows, and I had my golf cart loaded with boxes of toilet paper, a mop, cleaning supplies, and of course my trusty plunger.

I would visit each restroom and go stall to stall to stall, often thinking, "Don't any of these kids know how to flush?!" Occasionally I would open a stall door and feel my stomach churn as I saw what wasn't flushed, and in all likelihood couldn't be flushed without assistance. Sometimes I'd have an internal dialogue with myself like, "This is just too gross, so I'm going to leave it for someone else," or "I could pretend I didn't see this one," or "I've done enough tonight already, so what's it going to hurt if I leave just this one?"

It was at these moments when I'd walk back to my golf cart, grab my trusty plunger, hold it high in the air, and literally say out loud, "This is a job for Plunger Maaaaan!"

And then I would swoosh back into the restroom to attack the problem, all while trying not to gag.

I wanted to serve the servants. I wanted to do what I could to show them how much I appreciated their needful but disgusting responsibilities. Sheep are messy, and cleaning up the messes will do more to cure a case of "That's beneath me" than anything else. Just like Jesus declared to His Father, "I wish there was another way, but nevertheless, not My will, but Your will be done." If Jesus could that for me, I can certainly clean up after some messy sheep.

Did I like being Plunger Man? No, not really, but I loved my team, so I loved serving them. We can do a lot of distasteful things because of the love we have for the sheep God has placed under our care.

I'm not suggesting that you take on the role of your organization's custodian, unless God has called you to do that. What I am advocating is that if you lean toward the pole of confidence, you must find ways to deliberately and consistently take on those things that will add humility to your confidence. Your attitude adjustment will be continuous; it's never a one-and-done action. You can mature by daily making the deliberate choices that will keep your confidence counterbalanced with a healthy dose of humility, and in so doing, you will connect with even more of the sheep under your care.

A mark of a godly shepherd leader is one who is confidently humbled that God has a call on his life.

5

A HUMBLE LEADER'S ATTITUDE ADJUSTMENT

The very essence of leadership
is that you have to have vision;
you can't blow an uncertain trumpet.
—*Theodore Hesburgh*

Now, let's talk about how the humble leader can add the confidence that will bring about the balance that is needed to lead well.

This is a tough one to discuss, because to those who are looking at a leader only from a distance, it would appear that humility is more godly than confidence. So many times I have seen a confident leader take a stand, only to have someone quote to him or her, "God opposes the proud." But pride really has nothing to do with whether we are wired by God to be naturally more confident or naturally more humble. Both the proud and the humble can have a self-promoting attitude; it's just that the confident person does it more openly than the humble person does.

Check this out: "Now Moses was a very humble man, more humble than anyone else on the face of the earth" (Numbers 12:3). Who wrote the book of Numbers? If you answered "Moses," you are correct. Doesn't that sound a bit brash to declare that you are more humble than anyone else on the earth? Yet, God allowed Moses to pen those words, making that a Holy Spirit-inspired statement of fact. Humility is a double-edged sword: it can serve a leader well when it is balanced with appropriate confidence, but it is a detriment to an organization's health if it is self-debasing humility that undercuts a leader's credibility.

Pumping Up the Humility

Those who tend toward being naturally humble can benefit from looking at those words of C.S. Lewis again: "Humility isn't thinking less of yourself; it's thinking of yourself less." Humility is a tremendous asset in shepherd leadership, but taken to an extreme without the proper counterbalance of confidence can cause the leader to think too little of herself. As a result, she will be reluctant to speak up when the sheep need a clear voice.

One well-known proverb says, "Without vision, the people perish" (Proverbs 29:18). Another translation of this verse says that without a confident, clear vision, people "cast off restraint." Shepherd leaders need to give clear direction and bold confidence to help their sheep move toward the God-given vision. The timid voice of one who thinks less of herself will not help anyone.

Just as the overly confident leader needs to add deliberate activities that will allow humility to grow, the overly humble leader needs to take deliberate steps to stoke the fires of confidence. Remember that simple phrase: "God chose me." Those who tend toward humility must find a way to remind themselves—and possibly re-remind themselves—"I'm in this shepherd leadership position because God placed me here."

The board was making a major decision. They were considering a change in their leadership to one who had completely different credentials and training from all of their previous leaders. Because this change would be so momentous, the board interviewed me for more than four hours. When they finally felt they had deliberated long enough, they asked me to leave the room while they prayed and voted. I stepped out into the lobby for just a couple of minutes when the door opened again and they asked me to step back inside.

"Well, Craig," the spokesman began, "we prayed and we feel you are the one God has selected for this position." I told them I would be happy to accept their offer. After they prayed over me, I began to pack up my things to head home.

"Hold on a minute," one of the board members said to me, "we're about to discuss the budget, and we think it would be good for you to be a part of this discussion." I agreed and resumed my seat at the table.

I was handed both the year-to-date financial report and the projected income and expenses for the remaining quarter of the year. "As you can see," the treasurer began, "we are projecting a $70,000 loss for this year." Then he turned to me and asked, "What are you going to do about that?"

I gulped, tried not to show that my stomach was doing flips, and said, "Honestly, I don't know." I paused, and since no one else said anything, I continued, "But I'll let you know what we come up with."

All the way home, I kept thinking, "What have I gotten myself into? I'm walking away from a successful business to oversee an organization that's going to go bankrupt before I even get started?!" But then I began to remind myself of something else: God chose me.

When I returned home, I immediately went to my journal. I flipped to the page where I had written down all of the reasons why I had concluded that God chose me for this position. I looked at the way God had spoken to me and to my wife, and the way friends who knew nothing about this decision spoke a confirming word to me. I looked at the pages where I had written down the vision I believed God had given me for this new organization, and how the board chairman's handwritten vision for the organization matched mine thought-for-thought. Looking at these words—at the specific dates and ways God had spoken, and confirmed, and re-confirmed His direction— gave me the confidence to step into this assignment, even when facing such a huge financial mountain.

I see something similar in the life of a man named John. He began preaching in the wilderness of Israel, and people flocked to hear him. He was confident in speaking God's Word, not equivocating at all even when speaking to Roman soldiers, religious leaders, or the king of Israel. But when he thought about his standing, his humility took over. When he looked to the coming of the Messiah, he said, "I'm not even worthy to take off His sandal."

So when Jesus the Messiah came to John and asked John to baptize Him, John's overriding humility was almost his undoing:

> *Then Jesus went from Galilee to the Jordan River to be baptized by John. But John tried to talk Him out of it. "I am the one who needs to be baptized by You," he said, "so why are You coming to me?"* (Matthew 3:13–14 NLT)

John was thinking less of himself, but he should have been thinking of himself less. This wasn't about John—it was about Jesus. Look at how Jesus replied to John: "It should be done, for we must carry out all that God requires" (v. 15 NLT). Another translation has Jesus saying that His baptism would "fulfill all righteousness."

Jesus came to be our High Priest. One of the requirements for the priest was "he must bathe himself in water" before he puts on the ceremonial robes that were to be worn in the tabernacle (Leviticus 16:4). Jesus also came to be our perfect sacrifice, so He needed to be like us in every single way (Hebrews 2:17). If John had been overly reliant on his humility and refused to baptize Jesus, these important prophecies would not have been able to "fulfill *all* righteousness."

John's birth was a miracle (Luke 1:5–25). Before he was even conceived, an angel told his father Zechariah that John "will be great in the sight of the Lord" and that he would "make ready a people prepared for the Lord." After John was born, Zechariah was filled with the Holy Spirit and prophesied over John:

> And you, my child, will be called a prophet of the Most High; for you will go on before the Lord to prepare the way for Him, to give His people the knowledge of salvation through the forgiveness of their sins, because of the

tender mercy of our God, by which the rising sun will come to us from heaven to shine on those living in darkness and in the shadow of death, to guide our feet into the path of peace. (Luke 1:76–79)

Since Luke penned these words long after these events took place, it is quite obvious that these prophetic words of Zechariah were written down at the time they were spoken. In essence, they became John's journal. When he felt his humility was making him less sure of himself, wondering why—or even *if*—God had really called him to this, he could go back and read his father's words. He could hear his mother and father recount to him how his birth miraculously came about. He could be re-reminded, "God chose me."

So if you tend toward humility, I would recommend you begin keeping a journal. Date each entry when you write down the Scripture you were reading, or the word of confirmation from a trusted friend, or the miraculous ways God showed you His plan for your life. Then when you are second-guessing your shepherd leadership role, wondering if it's right for you to speak out or act with more boldness, you can return to these journal entries and say out loud, "I know God chose me for this." The more often you can remind yourself that God placed you in your leadership position for such a time as this, the more you will feel your confidence grow.

As I said in the previous chapter, this attitude adjustment is continuous; it's never done until God calls you home. If you tend toward the pole of humility, that's because God made you that way on purpose. Will you listen to the Holy Spirit's words of balance? You can see noticeable growth in your leadership maturity by daily making the deliberate choices that will add confidence to your humility.

A mark of a godly shepherd leader is one who is humbly confident that God has a call on his life.

6

STICK-TO-IT-IVENESS

This, then, is how you ought to regard us:
as servants of Christ and as those entrusted
with the mysteries God has revealed.
—*Paul of Tarsus*

If adding humility to our confidence or confidence to our humility requires a continuous action, how much more so does staying motivated to be the shepherd leader God has called us to be. Let's be honest: caring for sheep is frequently a thankless role. Just as soon as they are brought to a green pasture, some of them decide they don't like this particular pasture, or the water is too cold, or they would rather be with another shepherd. The long hours that shepherds put in are only rarely recognized by the sheep, and often the sheep ask why the shepherd wasn't available more.

This is the reason why shepherd leaders need to be secure in our simple statement: "God chose me." If God chose you for this role, He also equipped you for this role. And if He equipped you for this role, He also expects a return on His investment. This security of God's calling and equipping and the weighty understanding of bringing to God a return on His investment should be our motivators to help us stick with our joyful responsibility.

No Pity Parties, Please

All my life I've been a multitasker. I'm always trying to find ways to leverage as much as I can out of the time I have. One of my little tricks is to try to get as many of my morning rituals done in the shower as I can, so I frequently take both my toothbrush and my razor with me.

One particular morning I was in the shower when my wife walked into our bathroom and said, "Hey, you left the cap off the toothpaste and you left the toothpaste tube on the counter. You never do that. What's up?"

What was up is that I was having a pity party. It was Saturday morning, and I was in the shower earlier than expected because of a phone call I had just received. We had an important event happening in another city that was going to require about a two-hour drive for me. As of Friday night, I had my Saturday all mapped out: I knew when I would get up, when I would leave for this event, what was going to happen at the event, and when I would get back home. I knew that I would still have some "me time" when I got back home on this beautiful Saturday.

But then I got the early morning phone call: "Sorry, but I can't make it today. I have an opportunity to go to the beach with some friends, so we're taking off in just a few minutes to spend the day there."

"What about your responsibilities at our event today?" I asked, trying to hide my annoyance at his selfishness. "Have you found anyone to fill in for you?"

"Oh, I kinda forgot about that," he said.

I paused, hoping he was going to add something like, "Never mind what I just said. I know I told you I'd be there to help, so I'll postpone my beach plans to honor my commitment." Instead, what I actually heard him say was, "My bad. Have a good day," and then he hung up.

This now meant that not only would I have to leave earlier in the morning, but there was also no way I would get back home for my "me time," let alone get back home with enough energy to do anything with my family.

Thus the pity party began.

I sulked into the bathroom with my toothbrush and my razor. I put toothpaste on my brush and was about to put the cap back on when I deliberately stopped and left both the cap and the tube on the bathroom counter, and then I gloomily climbed into the shower.

"What's up?" my wife asked.

"I left it that way on purpose," I pouted. "Apparently, that is the only place in my life where I'm allowed any irresponsibility."

My wife put the cap on the toothpaste and returned the tube to the bathroom drawer. Then she lovingly asked me, "Are you going to let your pity party ruin your entire day? Are you going to let one person's action rain on everyone who is going to attend today? If you leave here under a cloud, you're going to bring that cloud with you. Is that fair to everyone else?"

And then she dropped this on me before walking out of the bathroom: "Your attitude is going to affect everyone at that event today. I hope you can make it a positive one."

To bring the positive attitude that is going to create a healthy environment for the sheep that we care for, we need to be secure in this: God chose me, God equipped me, and God expects a return on His investment.

We Are Under-Shepherds

One of the things that is extremely helpful to the stick-to-it-iveness of shepherd leaders—especially in those times we may be battling a pity party—is to remember that we are under-shepherds who are accountable to the Good Shepherd. This means that we don't have to figure out on our own how to care for the sheep, because the Good Shepherd knows them better than we do, and He will share His insight with us. Neither do we need to learn the shepherding ropes on our own, because both God the Father (the Shepherd of Israel) and Jesus the Son have already demonstrated for us all that we need to do, and the Holy Spirit will continually impart to us the ways we can apply those practices to our particular sheepfold.

Jesus called on Peter to be an under-shepherd who would take care of God's flock that was under his care. Peter lived this out so consistently that near the end of his life he used the imagery of a shepherd when he said:

> *Be shepherds of God's flock that is under your care, watching over them—not because you must, but because you are willing, as God wants you to be; not pursuing dishonest gain, but eager to serve; not lording it over those entrusted to you, but being examples to the flock. And when the Chief Shepherd appears, you will receive the crown of glory that will never fade away.* (1 Peter 5:2–4)

Notice that Peter calls these precious people "God's flock" and says that they have been placed "under your care." It really changes our perspective when we think of the people we lead as God's people and not "my people," doesn't it? They are simply sheep "entrusted to you."

Peter also talks to us about our attitude. Can you hear the no-pity-party admonition when he says, "not because you must, but because you are willing"? Back in chapter 2, I quoted the words of Jeremiah to his faithful servant Baruch: "Do you seek great things for yourself? Do not seek them." Let me give you the context for this. Baruch had faithfully obeyed God and faithfully stood by Jeremiah, but now that the heat was on, he was having a bit of a pity party: "Woe is me now! For the Lord has added grief to my sorrows. I fainted in my sighing and find no rest" (Jeremiah 45:1–5). In essence, Baruch was saying, "Things are not working out as *I* had planned." Jeremiah reminds Baruch that we don't serve as under-shepherds for our benefit, but for the benefit of God's sheep. Peter goes on to remind us that God wants us to be both willing to serve and "eager to serve," which means that correcting a sour attitude is something we need to quickly address.

Finally, Peter instructs us that our example for the flock must be God-honoring. People do what people see. If I would have arrived on that Saturday bent out of shape that things weren't working out as *I* had planned, I would have robbed people of the enjoyment that they should have had that day. Remember that when Jesus told us that He had set an example for us (John 13:15), it was an example of putting others' needs ahead of His own. Did Jesus want to wash those dirty feet? Probably not. But He not only washed them well, but He also had such a good attitude that its impact is still being felt today.

Peter was there on that day. He heard Jesus say this about following His example of such others-focused leadership: "Now that you know these things, you will be blessed if you do them." So Peter reminds his readers that the Chief Shepherd is returning with rewards for the faithful under-shepherds. Occasionally, we will get some rewards here, but keeping our steadfast focus on the rewards and blessings that are still to come will help us stick with our responsibilities, even on those days when no one else seems to notice or even care.

Talents from the Chief Shepherd

Regardless of your feelings about Rush Limbaugh, he frequently made a profound statement about having "talent on loan from God." This isn't true just for Mr. Limbaugh, but also for every single person that God has chosen to be in a place of leadership.

In Matthew 25, we hear Jesus telling us about talents that the master of the house gave to his servants. I realize that a "talent" in this case is an amount of money, but I don't think we stretch the point too far if we say that "talent" can be actual talents—gifts, abilities, insights, and wisdom—that our Master has given to His under-shepherds. In this story that Jesus related, the master expected a return on his investment: he expected to get back more than he gave (vv. 14–30).

There is no break in Christ's teaching as He proceeds to explain what a return on investment looks like: feeding the hungry, giving water to the thirsty, showing hospitality to the stranger, clothing the naked, caring for the sick, and visiting the prisoner (vv. 31–46). Doesn't this sound similar to the way the Good Shepherd cares for us, as David relates it in Psalm 23?

Jesus expressed a similar thought in Luke's gospel when He said, "Who then is the faithful and wise manager, whom the master puts in charge of his servants to give them their food allowance at the proper time? It will be good for that servant whom the master finds doing so when he returns" (Luke 12:42–43).

Jesus made it clear that under-shepherds shouldn't expect very many rewards or even accolades on this side of heaven (see Luke 17:7–10). In fact, we should be so eager to serve, so focused on giving our Chief Shepherd a fantastic return on His investment, that we don't even have time to stop to wonder if people are applauding or not.

Under-shepherds need to control their attitude, not letting it slip into pity-party mode. We need to make sure our attitude is always "eager to serve," not for temporary rewards here, but for eternal rewards from our Master in heaven. We can stick with this servant-hearted attitude if we will remember God has called us to this role, and He has equipped us for it.

Perhaps we could adapt the 23rd Psalm about the Good Shepherd to our own attitude-correcting, security-building prayer:

Because You are my Chief Shepherd, I lack nothing that is needed to care for the sheep You have placed under my care.

Just as You provide food for me in green pastures, and quiet waters for my thirst, I am equipped to feed the hungry and give drink to the thirsty.

You continually refresh my soul, so I can offer refreshing hospitality to those who have been beat up along life's journey.

You guide me along the right paths for Your name's sake, so I can show others the path into Your presence.

Even when I walk through the darkest valleys, I never fear because You are with me; You comfort me and provide all that I need so that I can care for the sick, the downhearted, and the weary without ever lapsing into my own pity party.

You continually prepare a table before me, even when I'm in the midst of enemies. You have anointed my head with oil and caused my cup of blessing to overflow, so I have more than enough to share with others.

I am secure that Your goodness and Your love will follow me all the days of my life, so I am equipped to lead others to the place where they too will dwell in Your house forever.

7

HERE'S TO YOUR HEALTH

Sometimes the most spiritual thing
I can do is go to bed early.
—*Eddie Tabor*

Shepherds are going to have an extremely difficult time leading their sheep anywhere if they are not at their optimal health. Notice that Jesus told us that He "did not come to be served, but to serve, and to give his life as a ransom for many" (Matthew 20:28). It's hard to serve when you aren't feeling well, and you cannot give to others what you don't possess yourself.

In chapter 3, William Deane's description of a shepherd depicts one who is constantly available to his sheep. Look at the ministry of the Chief Shepherd Jesus and the demands on His time. But it is even in His busy days that we can learn how Christ's health enabled Him to be available for the sheep that needed His attention.

A Doctor's Observations

One of the special people God used to record Scripture for us is a man named Luke. He was a trained doctor. Probably initially trained as a family's personal physician, he obviously continued his education beyond medicine because he also made himself into a first-rate historian. As both a doctor and historian, he naturally noticed things that others would miss. Luke gives us two observations that are highly instructive in his record of the early life of Jesus.

The first insight is: "And the Child [Jesus] grew and became strong in spirit, filled with wisdom; and the grace of God was upon Him" (Luke 2:40). The word Dr. Luke uses for "grew" means a continual process of increasing. In other words, there wasn't a supernatural growth that Jesus experienced, but He grew just as you and I do. This is further brought out when the writer of Hebrews tells us that Jesus experienced every aspect of human life that we will have to experience ourselves (Hebrews 2:14, 17).

Then for the phrase "became strong," Dr. Luke uses a word that means that Jesus was taking everything He was learning and putting it to productive use. In fact, both verbs are in the imperfect tense to signal that it was an ongoing process.

The second insight essentially covers all of Christ's developing years from ages twelve to thirty: "And Jesus grew in wisdom and stature, and in favor with God and man" (Luke 2:52). In this observation, the word "grew" is a different Greek medical word that means to be hammer out, as a blacksmith hammers metal. Notice that Jesus is not doing the fashioning, but He is submitting to the fashioning. In essence, Jesus is the metal and His Father is the blacksmith.

Notice how Dr. Luke lists four areas of growth. He says that Jesus grew in:

1. wisdom—mental health
2. stature—physical health
3. favor with God—spiritual health
4. favor with men—emotional (or social) health

In other words, Jesus was growing in a wholly healthy way. All four areas are vital. All four areas need attention. In all four areas, we need to be submitted to the Blacksmith.

A deficiency in any one of the areas can become a disease (or maybe we could call it a "dis-ease"). If even just one area is at dis-ease, it will affect *all* the other areas. For example, if we aren't growing in the area of wisdom, we will make poor choices for our physical health and we will have difficulty understanding and applying God's Word in our spiritual life. These two deficiencies can negatively impact our emotions and our social interactions with others.

Or what about if we are physically tired? It becomes challenging to think clearly and gain wisdom, we can't stay awake to pray so our spiritual life is stunted, and in our exhaustion we become short-tempered or easily hurt by others, and again our social interactions suffer as a result.

Do you see any of these deficiencies or areas of dis-ease in Jesus? His mind was sharp, as He could quickly recall passages of Scripture or answer a tricky question. We don't read of Him having any physical weaknesses that made Him say, "Sorry, I can't walk to that village today." His spiritual life was so in-tune with His heavenly Father that God Himself said, "This is My Son in Whom I am well pleased." And in His social interactions with others, Jesus never misspoke where He had to go back to apologize. He was wholly healthy, which allowed Him to be the perfect Chief Shepherd.

The Health of Sheep

Sheep, on the other hand, need almost constant attention if they are going to remain healthy. Remember we said earlier that shepherds cannot reproduce more sheep, but they are responsible to create the environment where healthy sheep can reproduce healthy sheep. As Psalm 23 tells us, the sheep need the shepherd to point them to the best pastures, to take them to the best water, to comfort them when they are frightened, and to apply soothing medicine to wounds. As God did for Israel, we under-shepherds will also have to carry the sheep at times: "He will gather the lambs in His arm, He will carry them in His bosom and will gently lead those that have their young" (Isaiah 40:11).

Jesus said that His mission was to the "lost sheep of Israel" (Matthew 15:24), and that like a loving physician He would care for the sick (Mark 2:17). In fulfilling the Old Testament prophecy, Jesus would meet the needs of the people gently and lovingly (Isaiah 42:3). To fulfill all of these shepherding responsibilities, Jesus would need to be wise, physically healthy, spiritually mature, and emotionally resilient.

Our Chief Shepherd has set the example for all His under-shepherds to follow. Can you hear the wholeness and healthiness that John desires for his friend Gaius?

Dear friend, I pray that you may enjoy good health and that all may go well with you, even as your soul is getting along well. It gave me great joy when some believers came and testified about your faithfulness to the truth, telling how you continue to walk in it. I have no greater joy than to hear that my children are walking in the truth. Dear friend, you are faithful in what you are doing for the brothers and sisters. (3 John 1:2–5)

Our mental, physical, spiritual, and emotional health are among the talents God has given us, talents that He expects us to use well so that there is a good return on His investment. We dare not be slack in any of these areas. Robert Murray McCheyne was given a special anointing to minister to his countrymen, but he undertook his ministry responsibilities in an irresponsible way, working himself to total exhaustion. As he lay on his deathbed at only twenty-nine years of age, he said to his friends, "The Lord gave me a horse to ride and a message to deliver. Alas, I have killed the horse and I cannot deliver the message."

As my friend Eddie Tabor said to me, "Sometimes the most spiritual thing I can do is go to bed early." How true that is! Sadly, many leaders who are struggling with an area of dis-ease know exactly why they are struggling, but they make excuses, such as "I'm just so busy" or "I can put my head down and power through this." These excuses keep them from making the necessary corrections. This inaction is slowly but surely robbing those shepherd leaders of vitality, and therefore robbing the sheep of the healthy environment that they need so they can reproduce.

Over the next five chapters, we are going to take some time to learn how leaders can assess their current health situation and then make simple changes that are vital to become wholly healthy shepherds. We need to get healthy not so much for ourselves, but for the sake of those under our care. Remember: you cannot give to others what you do not possess yourself. If you want a healthy flock, you as the shepherd leader must get healthy first.

8

IT ALL BEGINS
IN YOUR HEAD

The illiterate of the future are not those
who cannot read or write,
but those who cannot learn,
unlearn, and relearn.

—*Alvin Tofler*

Dr. Luke is a great "noticer." Twice he notices and records something about the early life of Jesus that gives shepherd leaders great insight to help them grow in a wholly healthy way. First of all, Luke tells us *how* Jesus grows (Luke 2:40), and then he begins to zero in on the four areas *in which* Jesus grew (Luke 2:52).

I'm intrigued by the order in which Luke lists the four areas of growth in the life of Jesus, because the order is significant. In our modern western world, we will often use numbered lists to show the level of importance of items, but authors in Luke's day didn't have the luxury of word processors or an abundance of paper, so they listed things in order of importance. For instance, throughout the Gospels when the disciples are listed by name, Peter is always listed first because he said more and had more said to him than any of the other disciples.

So notice the order in which Luke lists the areas of growth: mental, then physical, then spiritual, and finally relational. I don't know about you, but putting mental health first stands out to me, as does putting relational health at the pinnacle (but more about this topic in chapter 12).

The first thing Dr. Luke notes is Christ growing in wisdom. Jesus was a lifelong learner. Just take a quick glance through the four Gospels, and you will see His instant recall of Scripture, His awareness of the songs children sang, His understanding of cultural practices, His awareness of current events, and His knowledge of medical science, biology, and religious and civil law.

Knowledge is not the same thing as wisdom. In fact, lots of people have knowledge without ever having wisdom. But we have to remember that you cannot get wisdom without getting knowledge first. The Greek language has a couple of words for knowledge. First is *ginosko*, which could probably be best described as having head knowledge, possessing basic information, or believing that something is true. Then there is the Greek word *oida*, which is experiential knowledge.

Let me give you a quick example to illustrate these two types of knowledge. One time, my facilities team was overseeing the reinstallation of our zip line from our thirty-foot-high ropes course. This zip line stretched some 500 feet from the platform on top of the ropes course all the way down a big hill. After the zip line was replaced, our facilities guys **believed that** (ginosko) they had successfully connected the zip line. But only Phil **believed in** (oida) their work enough to put on a harness, connect to the zip line, and jump off the platform!

Before any mental growth can ever happen it is imperative that we have this understanding: I don't know everything. This humble admission can lead us to seek out the knowledge we are lacking, which can help us be more confident in the decisions we need to make. However, if our pride keeps us from admitting that we may be lacking knowledge, the outcome of our decisions could be disastrous or even fatal.

The Four Quadrants of Learning

Martin M. Broadwell first described how all of us go through four quadrants as we learn. We begin in an area called "unconscious incompetence." We aren't knowledgeable in a particular area, but we don't even know it. Some may refer to this as a blind spot. The Holy Spirit will lovingly make us aware of these blind spots if we ask Him to. I think this is why David prayed, "How can I know all the sins lurking in my heart? Cleanse me from these hidden faults" (Psalm 19:12 NLT).

When the light shines on this place of unconscious incompetence, we have a choice to make. We can deny our ignorance and put a lid on our leadership development, or we can humbly admit our need for help in this area and move into the next quadrant.

The next quadrant of growth is called "conscious incompetence," because we now know that we're deficient in an area. This is the place for setting learning goals or seeking a mentor who can help address this concern. I remember stepping into a leadership position where for the first time I had people from very diverse backgrounds in my circle of influence. As I would work alongside them and hear about some of their struggles, I quickly realized how little information I had with which to help them. It was then I made a conscious decision to modify my reading list to include books that would help me help my teammates.

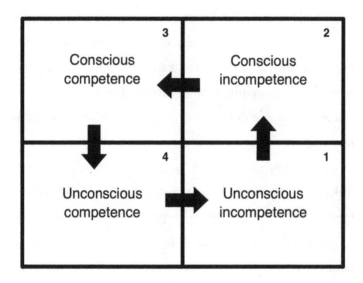

There is an important note of caution for this second quadrant. As you begin to learn and apply things you didn't know before, you will undoubtedly begin doing things that you haven't done before. With this comes a sense of awkwardness, and with this awkwardness comes the temptation to want to return to the way you did things previously. But remember that just because it doesn't feel natural to you, that doesn't mean it's ineffective. You will need to persevere through this awkwardness so that you can get to the third quadrant.

Quadrant three is called "conscious competence." In this area, because you have persevered, things are beginning to feel a bit more natural to you, but you still find yourself thinking carefully before you speak or act. This is a good place to be! You are creating new pathways in your brain with the new knowledge you have. Don't ever buy into that old adage, "You can't teach an old dog new tricks." Neuroscientists have shown that our brains can remain malleable until the day we die—we can always be learning new things.

Ultimately, as you stick with your new learning, you move into the final quadrant called "unconscious competence." Here you have gotten so good in an area that you no longer need to think about it because it's become second nature to you. This is where your knowledge has truly become what we can call wisdom.

Again, there is one danger in this fourth quadrant that I need to point out. Notice that both the first and fourth quadrants have the word "unconscious" in them. This means that good things in quadrant four can quickly become the blind habits of "we've always done it this way" of quadrant one. We can slip from things being unconsciously competent to unconsciously incompetent if we are not always vigilant. This underscores the need for us to remain life-long learners.

Solomon used the word "prudent" to describe the one who is aware of his surroundings, even aware of his own areas of incompetence, and is therefore quickly addressing them before they become a detriment to himself or others. Solomon said such things as:

> The prudent understand where they are going, but fools deceive themselves. (Proverbs 14:8 NLT)

> A prudent person foresees danger and takes precautions. The simpleton goes blindly on and suffers the consequences. (Proverbs 22:3 NLT)

I think this way of growing through all four of the quadrants is wonderfully captured in this poem from Portia Nelson:

I walk down the street.
There is a deep hole in the sidewalk.
I fall in.
I am lost ... I am helpless. It isn't my fault.
It takes forever to find a way out.

I walk down the same street.

There is a deep hole in the sidewalk.

I pretend I don't see it.

I fall in, again.

I can't believe I am in the same place. But it isn't my
    fault.

I walk down the same street.

There is a deep hole in the sidewalk.

I see it is there.

I still fall in ... it's a habit ... but my eyes are open,
    I know where I am.

It's my fault. I get out immediately.

I walk down the same street.

There is a deep hole in the sidewalk.

I walk around it.

I walk down another street.

Practical and Heavenly

The Greek word Dr. Luke uses for the way Jesus grew
mentally is *sophia*. Have you ever heard someone say, "He's
so heavenly minded that he's no earthly good"? Wouldn't
it be just as true of some people that they are so earthly
minded that they are no heavenly good? But I don't think

anyone would use either of these phrases to describe Jesus! Jesus was both heavenly minded and earthly practical.

In practical and God-honoring ways, Jesus went from *ginosko* to *oida* to *sophia*. He learned new things, unlearned things that were tied to traditions or not supported by God's Word, and then relearned God's way of living. Only shepherd leaders that are continually progressing through all four quadrants of learning are gaining both the solid information and practical, God-honoring wisdom that they can use to grow themselves. And it's only shepherds who are continually turning healthy knowledge into God-honoring, practical wisdom that can create a healthy environment for their sheep in ever-changing cultures. Wise shepherds know how to adapt to threats, to prepare for the unexpected, to overcome the old traditions, and to lead their sheep safely to the healthy places.

Those leaders who aren't lifelong learners aren't open to allowing the Holy Spirit to consistently show them areas of deficiency. They rob themselves of health in every area of their lives. Remember that all four area of health—mental, physical, spiritual, relational—are inter-connected. Deficiency in one area can lead to inefficiency and ultimately dis-ease in all of the areas. When we allow the Holy Spirit to constantly help us grow in *sophia*, we're allowing harmony to reign in all four areas of our lives.

Shepherd, your healthy growth as a leader is directly tied to the continual way you are turning knowledge into wisdom. Your health has a direct impact on the health of the flock under your care. It's a part of your stewardship to be a lifelong learner. Let's give Jesus the final word on this:

You've been given insight into God's kingdom. You know how it works. Not everybody has this gift, this insight; it hasn't been given to them. Whenever someone has a ready heart for this, the insights and understandings flow freely. But if there is no readiness, any trace of receptivity soon disappears. That's why I tell stories: to create readiness, to nudge the people toward receptive insight. In their present state they can stare till doomsday and not see it, listen till they're blue in the face and not get it. I don't want Isaiah's forecast repeated all over again: "Your ears are open but you don't hear a thing. Your eyes are awake but you don't see a thing. The people are blockheads! They stick their fingers in their ears so they won't have to listen; they screw their eyes shut so they won't have to look, so they won't have to deal with Me face-to-face and let Me heal them." (Matthew 13:11–15, MSG)

9

A HEALTHY
SHEPHERD'S SABBATH

Working 41—48 hours a week instead
of a "normal" 35—40 raises your risk of stroke by 10 percent;
toiling 49—54 hours ups it by 27 percent; and slaving away for
55 hours hoists it by a shocking 33 percent.
—Men's Health Magazine

Anyone in a ministry position, anyone who has to help hurting people, knows that his ministry isn't restricted to a "normal" forty-hour work week. In fact, it's even hard to keep a consistent day off. Far too many ministry leaders blindly accept that there is nothing they can do about this, and they allow their shepherding duties to utterly consume them to the point of burnout.

This is why Dr. Luke lists the growth of Jesus' mind as first importance. We have to gain wisdom and then use this hard-won wisdom to make healthy physical, spiritual, and relational decisions. I don't know about you, but many of my "Aha!" moments have come after going through a painful experience. I suspect you have had similar experiences. I also suspect that you would rather not have to go through the pain to learn those lessons. This is why being a lifelong learner is so valuable. For instance, reading biographies of great leaders of the past will allow you to learn lessons from their lives without having the painful experiences yourself. You are letting their hindsight be your foresight. This is also true when we read the Bible: there are invaluable lessons that we can glean from the painful choices or inactions of so many biblical characters.

Moving closer to today, with easy access via the Internet, there really isn't any excuse for us to not read about the latest medical studies that can keep our physical bodies healthy and strong. Shepherds definitely need to be physically strong—strong enough to stay up all night with a grieving family, strong enough to pray with a friend struggling with an addiction or a failing marriage, strong enough to battle the enemies of God's flock, strong enough to have extraordinary patience when a hurting sheep pushes your buttons.

We have to learn and apply healthy habits. As James told us, "Remember, it is sin to know what you ought to do and then not do it" (James 4:17).

Jesus Was Strong

If you asked others to give you descriptions of Jesus, I wonder how many of those portraits might mention His physical strength. The carpentry work He did during His early years in Nazareth undoubtedly toned His muscles, but have you ever noticed what isn't mentioned in the Gospels? We never read of Jesus being too tired or too weak to help someone who was in need.

And most important of all, ponder the ramifications of this question: What if Jesus hadn't been strong enough to make it to the top of Calvary's hill?

Think about the excruciating torture Jesus went through: He was sleep deprived, He was dehydrated from His intense prayer time in Gethsemane where He sweat blood, He was beaten up multiple times by the temple guards and Roman soldiers, He was brutally whipped to the point that His back muscles and nerves were exposed, He had thorns crushed into His scalp, He had His beard ripped out, and then He had to carry a 60-pound wooden crossbeam nearly 650 yards uphill!

All of this took place *before* He even had the metal spikes slammed through His wrists and ankles, and He was hoisted up rudely into the air to be suspended from the Cross. All forgiven sinners are eternally grateful that Jesus went through all of that for us! In making it all the way to the point where He could say, "It is finished," Jesus fulfilled every prophecy that made our salvation possible.

But note this: The only way Jesus could have made it through all of this was if He was at optimal physical health. If Jesus had died from exhaustion or a heart attack or loss of blood before He was actually nailed to the Cross, how many of the prophecies would have been left unfulfilled? He needed to keep His physical body in tip-top shape throughout His entire earthly life to be ready for this one crucial moment.

Our physical health is no less important today. As His under-shepherds, we have to care for His sheep, attend to their needs whenever they are sick or hurting, search for lost sheep in the middle of the night, and remain vigilant against the attacks of the devil. If our physical health is run down, we can typically keep doing these tasks, but our patience will begin to wear thin and our effectiveness will begin to diminish. Being physically tired makes it difficult for us to concentrate and learn new things (mental health), be attentive to the things of God (spiritual health), and even control our emotions and respond appropriately to other people (relational health). So we, like Jesus, must work on our physical health.

Fortunately, Jesus set us an example even in this area.

Sabbathing

Shepherd leaders tend to feel as if they must always be "on"—always ready for the next need that may arise. But in order to be "on" in a healthy way, we have to be "off" in a healthy way, too.

Consider the public ministry of Jesus. His mission was to prepare His followers to take the message of salvation to the entire planet, and He had about thirty-three years to accomplish that. We know next to nothing about the first thirty years of His life because the Gospels essentially record only the final three years, the years of His public ministry. Of these three years of ministry—roughly 1,277 days—only about 35 days are recorded for us. You might expect that these days would be filled with furious activity from sunrise to sunset, and perhaps even through the midnight hours as well.

But let's look at just the beginning of the Gospel of Mark. I'm choosing this Gospel because of the way Mark jumps right into the action without any mention of the birth of Jesus. Mark also uses such words as "immediately" and "right away" more than the other Gospel writers. And yet in just the first six chapters, we don't see anything like "Go, go go!" about the ministry of Jesus. Instead, we see Him spending forty days alone with His Father in the desert (Mark 1:12–13), eating dinner at Peter and Andrew's house (1:29), getting up for an early-morning prayer time (1:35), having dinner with Matthew and his coworkers (2:15), going for a long walk with His disciples (2:23), and heading back home to see His family (6:1).

Jesus had a human body just like ours. The demands of ministry caused stress on His body just as it does on our bodies. This is totally natural—this is the way God designed us. Our body helps us meet the demands of each day by releasing a hormone called *cortisol*. Cortisol helps us by managing how our body uses carbohydrates, fats, and proteins; keeping inflammation down; regulating blood pressure; controlling the sleep-wake cycle; and boosting our energy. Cortisol is naturally flushed out of our body each day by exercise and rest.

But what happens if we don't have the proper exercise and rest? In that case, cortisol can become a cruel boomerang, leading to unhealthy weight loss or gain, inflammation (and the accompanying aches and pains), elevated blood pressure, difficulty sleeping at night, and difficulty staying awake during the day. As a result, we start to turn every molehill into a mountain, and we tend to the extremes of avoiding or arguing, what we might call fight or flight.

Cortisol is naturally flushed from our bodies by a healthy on-and-off rhythm. God built this into His Creation by giving us daily rhythms of day and night, work and rest, and by providing a weekly Sabbath to rest and reflect. But as most shepherd leaders know, setting aside a consistent Sabbath day is extremely rare. Again, let's look to Jesus: Do you see Him doing anything—or not doing anything—on the Sabbath day that He didn't do the other days? On any day of the week, we see Him speaking in a synagogue, healing the sick, teaching crowds of people, giving instructions to His followers, correcting religious leaders, walking with friends, or stopping to eat at someone's home.

Jesus had a healthy on-off rhythm: work-rest, minister-celebrate, expend-refresh. Jesus demonstrated that the Sabbath is not so much a day as it is an attitude of the heart. It's listening to the Holy Spirit say something like, "You've been very busy this afternoon, so it's time to take a nap" and then obeying that divine prompting. Resting and being refreshed—"sabbathing"—is not a luxury; it's a necessity! That's why, after a busy day of ministry, we see Jesus spending time in prayer, or taking a nap while crossing the lake when He didn't have anyone to teach or heal, or finding time for a retreat with His disciples so they could rest and recuperate.

Without building in sabbath breaks, we run down emotionally, spiritually, mentally, and physically, which means loving God becomes of a chore, not a delight (Mark 12:30). This then means loving your neighbor becomes nearly impossible (Mark 12:31). Ultimately, this means that we aren't able to be the compassionate, wise, strong shepherds that the sheep under our care need us to be.

If you find yourself grouchy, unable to concentrate, unfocused in your prayer or Bible study time, or annoyed at the needs of yet another sheep, the root cause may be a lack of sabbathing. Let me repeat an important shepherding principle: You cannot give to the sheep what you do not possess yourself. If you want the sheep to be in a healthy place, you have to be in a healthy place.

I pray this prayer of John the Beloved for you: *"Dear friend, I pray that you may enjoy good health and that all may go well with you, even as your soul is getting along well"* (3 John 2). But I also pray that you will become increasingly sensitive to the voice of the Holy Spirit telling you how sabbathing can bring the good health to your physical body that both you and your sheep need.

So listen to His voice. Go to bed when you're tired, take time to eat the healthy food your body needs, stop to pray after you've been spiritually expended, make the time to exercise and recreate. And if you're wondering, "How in the world am I going to find time to take these sabbathing breaks?"—that's the subject of the very next chapter!

10

CAN'T, WON'T, OR DON'T

Sabbathing is absolutely vital to
your effectiveness and longevity
as a shepherd leader.
—Craig T. Owens

It is very instructive that Jesus began His three years of public ministry after thirty years of preparation, and that He began His daily ministry after an early-morning prayer session. At the end of His public ministry, Jesus said that every word He spoke was divinely directed, as was every action He performed. Clearly, His "off" time—that is, His time sabbathing out of sight—made His "on" time so much more effective.

Our physical health works much the same way: "off" makes "on" better, and "on" makes "off" sweeter. Or as medical doctors might say, your exercise increases the recuperative value of your sleep, and your sleep enables your exercise to be more effective. When we are consistently sabbathing, off-and-on will balance and enhance each other. Rest must follow work, or else soon the work will become ineffective. In fact, a deficiency of rest might result in a prolonged rest (illness) or even a permanent rest (death). Sabbathing is absolutely vital to your effectiveness and longevity as a shepherd leader.

Why Leaders Are Sabbath Deficient

There are three main attitudes that hinder our lack of sabbathing: can't, won't, and don't.

- "I *can't* sabbath because no one is available to step in to care for the sheep in my off time."
- "I *won't* sabbath because someone might step in to care for the sheep in my off time, and I will lose my place."
- "I *don't* sabbath because I don't know how to sabbath."

"Can't" is usually rooted in guilt that makes us believe we have to be constantly "on." Because of our love for the sheep under our care, we never want to leave them in a vulnerable place, but we simply don't see anyone else responsible enough to step up to care for them. As a result, we make ourselves always available because we fear letting anyone down.

My friend, if this is your attitude, let me tell you that I love your heart for the sheep! But let me also add another loving word: If you don't take time to effectively sabbath, eventually your love will begin to feel like a duty and not a delight. When your shepherding leadership is no longer delightful for you, trust me, everyone around you knows it. We'll look more closely at how to raise up more shepherds who can assist you in chapter 13, but let me encourage you even now to adapt a prayer that Jesus taught us to pray:

The opportunities for the sheep to flourish are great, as are the needs that the sheep have. So I ask the Chief Shepherd to send out more skilled and loving under-shepherds into the pastures where I care for these precious sheep. (adapted from Luke 10:1–3)

"Won't" is fueled by a subtle but hideous pride that keeps someone trapped by the idea that he is the one and only leader. The shepherd with this attitude never wants to allow others a chance to replace him. The thinking goes something like this: "What if everyone gets along fine without me? Will I be replaced? Will I lose my position?" But remember our simple statement: God chose me. God will keep you exactly where you need to be for as long as you need to be there. Neither success nor failure can remove you one minute before God is ready to remove you.

King Nebuchadnezzar believed he had successfully leveraged his talent and opportunities to make Babylon into a world power. Yet as he walked around surveying all of the outward signs of success, he said, "Look at all *I* have accomplished." This prideful attitude led to a temporary downfall. In the midst of this, Daniel reminded him, "The Most High is sovereign over all the kingdoms of the earth and He gives them to whom He chooses" (Daniel 4:25). It's not a stretch at all for us to restate that verse this way: The Chief Shepherd is sovereign over all the flocks of sheep on earth, and He gives them to the under-shepherds He chooses. My friend, God has placed you in your position, and He will keep you there or He will move you. That is His sovereign choice. Your unwillingness to listen to the Holy Spirit, who is telling you to take a sabbath rest, isn't going to keep your leadership secure. Whether you take a sabbath break or not, God is still in control over who will shepherd His sheep.

Remember in chapters 4 and 5 that we talked about strategies for confident leaders to grow their humility and humble leaders to grow their confidence. This practice of sabbathing is where this balance or imbalance is seen.

The leader with a "can't sabbath" attitude is actually giving in to the fear of what if: "What if something bad happens while I'm away? If something bad happens, I'll feel guilty, and the flock probably won't want me to stick around." This is an indication that confidence needs to be infused to add the counterbalance to humility.

Likewise, the leader with a "won't sabbath" attitude needs to add the counterbalance of humility to their "I'm-in-charge" confidence. We need to use the fear of the *can't* attitude or the pride of the *won't* attitude as warning signs of an imbalance, return to those earlier chapters, pray, and then let the Holy Spirit help us find that centered-point of confident humility or humble confidence.

The Holy Spirit is the best One to help us spot both the *can't* and *won't* attitudes. This is good counsel from Dave Adamson: "The Hebrew word for prayer—*tefillah*—means to self evaluate. So to the Jews of the Bible, prayer was not a time when they asked God for things ... it was a time when they examined themselves. They would use prayer as a way to compare their actions, behavior and attitude against God's holiness." Shepherd leaders need to have regular times of evaluation in God's presence to keep them from the fear that fuels the *can't* attitude or the pride that stokes the *won't* attitude.

Tick Tock

When our *can't* and *won't* attitudes are addressed, we are in a much better place to tackle the *don't know how to* attitude of sabbathing. This attitude is a great place to be! I've often said that the shortest and most powerful prayer is simply, "God, help!" In these two words, we're saying: "I don't know how to do this, but You do; I don't know where to turn, but You do; I can't do it on my own, but with You I'm unstoppable!" Let me give the really good news right up front: With this kind of attitude, making the time to consistently sabbath is going to be easier to implement than you might have previously thought.

Most of the time, we think of time passing by as a "Tick, Tock," but I would rather us think of time passing as "Drip, Drop." I've gotten some great insight on time usage from Paul Meyer like this one: "Most time is wasted, not in hours, but in minutes. A bucket with a small hole in the bottom gets just as empty as a bucket that is deliberately emptied."

Usually our time doesn't just Tick! by, it Drips! out. In other words, it's really easy to spot the huge time-wasters; it's much more difficult to find the time-leakers. But they can be found and plugged. Listen to one more piece of advice from Dr. Meyer: "Time is usually wasted in the same way every day." You cannot add more Tick, Tocking! time to your day, but you can keep more of your day from Drip, Dropping! away.

Here are four things I've done that have really helped me identify the drips. First, for one week—seven full days—I kept a log of how I spent every fifteen-minute increment. This might sound like a Drip, Drop! thing to do, but I was amazed at how many leaks I discovered during a week of doing this.

Second, I listed each of my activities in one of four categories that Stephen Covey created.

	Urgent	**Not Urgent**
Important	I	II
Not Important	III	IV

Quadrant I contains things that are both urgent and important. Urgent means they have a deadline or due date attached to them, and important means that they have high value for both me and the flock I shepherd.

Quadrant II things are important, high-value items that don't have a set time when they must be completed.

Quadrant III are those things that are demanding an immediate action (such as a ringing telephone) but may not be mission critical for me or the organizations I shepherd.

And Quadrant IV contains those things that are neither urgent nor important.

Third, after I listed the items I recorded in my journal of fifteen-minute increments onto this grid, I prayed the same prayer Moses prayed: "Give me wisdom to use my days the right way" (Psalm 90:12). After praying this "God, help!" prayer, I finally felt ready to begin to make the necessary changes.

Finally, I began to address the items on the grid to make time to regularly sabbath. The highest priority is to create more time in Quadrant II. This is really the only place where we have time for learning (mental health), exercise and diet (physical health), prayer and Bible study (spiritual health), and meaningful interactions with others (relational health). We sabbath in Quadrant II, and Quadrant II creates the health we need to care for our sheep.

The best place to create sabbathing time for Quadrant II is by removing things from Quadrant IV. Without a doubt, Quadrant IV is the biggest Drip, Drop offender! When I wrote things down in fifteen-minute increments, I found time wasters such as excessive social media usage, mindless surfing through TV channels or YouTube videos, and needless rabbit trails during my study time. If you want a real eye-opener on how much unproductive time is in Quadrant IV, try fasting from one of the items in this Quadrant for thirty days. For example, fasting from all social media gave me more time to read, pray, and exercise. After the month was up, I began to use social media again, but I now kept that activity on a very short leash.

Quadrants I and III are good places to involve other people. A Quadrant I activity for me is some of the financial reports that need to be prepared monthly or filed quarterly. The IRS has set a timeline on these forms, so that definitely qualifies it as an urgent activity, and knowing where we stand financially is definitely important. But since I'm not a "numbers guy," these tasks were both unfulfilling and took me way too long to complete. None of us are very effective in areas outside of our gift zone, so I've been blessed to have trusted people who are gifted in this area and enjoy working with those forms. They can oversee these tasks for me, freeing up time for me to spend in Quadrant II.

A Quadrant III activity might be responding to people who need to talk with me. I love talking with people, but I simply cannot respond to every call or text or email immediately. So I can recruit other team members or utilize technology to reassure these people that I will be in touch with them soon, but in the meantime there are others who can assist until I am available.

These things take time to fully implement, but I can tell you that I was better able to sabbath almost as soon as I began the first step of this journey. The goal of sabbathing is to infuse more vitality into the shepherd leader for the purpose of pasturing the sheep under that leader's care. You cannot give hope to others unless you are hope-filled; you cannot give health to others unless you are healthy; you cannot consistently speak wisdom to others unless you are growing in wisdom. All of this healthy growth for the shepherd leader takes place while sabbathing inside Quadrant II. This was the consistent lifestyle of the Chief Shepherd, and it must be so for us, too.

I know some of you may still be unconvinced that you should regularly sabbath. Perhaps you feel that this time for self-care is unnecessary. Let me leave you with a word that the Holy Spirit dropped in my heart as I was wrestling with consistency in my sabbathing: Self-care is not selfish; selfish is self-centered. Sabbathing is self-care; not sabbathing is both self-centered and shortsighted.

Consistency in sabbathing is a huge paradigm shift for most leaders, so it remains one of my most consistent prayers for you.

11

FOUR ELEMENTS
TO OPTIMAL
SPIRITUAL HEALTH

Health is not just a big one-time choice.
Health is small daily choices.
—*Josh Schram*

Every word of the Bible is inspired—things are plural on purpose, and there is a divine order in the way items are listed. Remember that Dr. Luke recorded the wholly healthy growth of Jesus in a very specific order: mental growth, physical growth, spiritual growth, relational growth. We need the mental know-how and how-to to grow in wisdom. We use this wisdom to develop the physical body that God gave us. The health of our mind and body helps create the environment where spiritual health can flourish. And ultimately our faith is lived out in relationship with other people.

We've seen how Jesus grew His mind and took care of His physical body, but now we come to these words: "Jesus grew ... in favor with God" (Luke 2:52). Jesus grew spiritually strong. Think about that—isn't He already God? How could God grow in favor with God?

When Jesus came to Earth as a Man, the writer of Hebrews says He was made like us humans *in every way* (Hebrews 2:17). So just as you and I have a spiritual health to maintain, so did Jesus while He was on earth. Jesus never stopped being God, but He chose not to use His divine prerogatives so that He would be able to empathize and help us. When the next verse of Hebrews says, "because He Himself suffered when He was tempted, He is able to help those who are being tempted," it literally means that He knows what our struggles feel like, and therefore He is able to intercede before God's throne of grace for our help.

So when Luke says that Jesus grew in favor with God, he is telling us that the Father was more and more pleased by what He saw developing in His Son.

Notice the Parallels

I'm struck by the parallels between maintaining physical health and maintaining spiritual health. When it comes right down to it, our physical health can be optimized by getting a handle on four key elements: (1) proper diet, (2) regular exercise, (3) appropriate rest and recovery, and

(4) regular times of evaluation and adjustment. Spiritual health is also optimized using these same four areas, and in many cases the Bible even uses the same words. As we discussed in the previous chapter, all of our proactive health-building disciplines are developed in Quadrant II. These are highly important habits for longevity and effectiveness in our shepherding duties, but they don't usually have a deadline attached to them.

Proper Diet

I think it's pretty straightforward that you cannot maintain any semblance of health without consuming a good diet. Notice above I used the word "proactive" with our daily health choices, because for the most part, those choices don't have a due date. However, if we neglect these choices for too long, our depleted health will force us to make reactive choices to get back on track.

A friend recently shared with me something his personal trainer said: "You cannot out-exercise a bad diet." How true that is! The fuel you put in your body is just as important as the fuel you put in your spirit. Remember John's desire for his beloved friend Gaius: "I pray that you may enjoy good health and that all may go well with you, even as your soul is getting along well" (3 John 2).

Jesus made it clear that His daily diet was the balanced nutrition of Scripture. When the devil attempted to trick

Jesus into overcoming His hunger in a way that would have required Jesus to use His divine prerogatives as God by turning stones into bread, Jesus quoted the Scripture, "Man does not live on bread alone but on every Word that comes from the mouth of the Lord" (Luke 4:4; compare Deuteronomy 8:1–3). Notice that even in Deuteronomy, Moses told us about the healthy daily decision to feast on God's Word:

> *Be careful to follow every command I am giving you today, so that you may live and increase.... [God] humbled you, causing you to hunger and then feeding you with manna, which neither you nor your ancestors had known, to teach you that man does not live on bread alone but on every word that comes from the mouth of the Lord.*
> (Deuteronomy 8:1, 3)

In grocery stores, gas stations, and convenience stores, junk food is not only more readily available than health food, but it is usually less expensive, too. It's more expensive to eat healthy, just as it's more "expensive" in terms of your time to linger in God's Word and in prayer. But the cumulative effects of our daily choices pay dividends down the road in either diminished health or enhanced health. Set aside the Quadrant II time every day to consume the healthy diet that is found only in Scripture.

Regular Exercise

If all I do is eat a healthy diet, but my exercise is insufficient, that healthy food can become counterproductive. All the health food in the world won't do us a bit of good if we just sit around. It's the same with the Bible: we can read it, memorize it, and talk about it, but if we don't exercise it, we won't get spiritually fit. This is why James instructs us, "Be doers [exercisers] of the Word, and not hearers [eaters] only" (James 1:22).

We have to work out what the Holy Spirit has worked in our hearts while we were eating the Scriptures. Or perhaps it's more accurate to say we have to let the Holy Spirit design the workout regimen our spirits need after we have consumed the spiritual food that will fuel our workouts. Once again, this choice to spiritually work out is a vitally important Quadrant II discipline.

The Greek word in the Bible translated "persevere" means keeping focused on the goal despite the struggles that it takes to get there. Jesus used this same Greek word at the conclusion of His parable of the sower: "The seed on good soil stands for those with a noble and good heart, who hear the Word, retain it, and by **persevering** produce a crop," a crop that Jesus said was a hundred times more than what was sown (see Luke 8:5–15). The Holy Spirit will push us farther than we think we can go to develop the spiritual muscles and endurance we need to shepherd the sheep under our care during their trying times. He knows that persevering produces a huge crop.

I love riding my bike on the White Pine Trail by my house. My long rides have a really fun stretch where I am flying downhill! But as fun as that part is, I'm not really building anything of lasting value. However, when I am coming back uphill and I want to quit because my legs are burning and I can hardly breathe, that becomes a valuable struggle. I cannot build endurance by any other way than to persevere, to push myself just a little bit more each time. When I want to quit, I pedal just a few more feet. Gradually, the uphill becomes less daunting.

A friend gave me a t-shirt that I like to wear on my rides. When I put the shirt on, the blue-lettered message says, "Do It!" but as I struggle uphill and the sweat begins to pour off my body and drench my shirt, a new message emerges: "Don't Quit!" I have learned that easy roads teach very few valuable lessons.

This is what Jesus demonstrated for us when "for the joy set before Him He endured the Cross" (Hebrews 12:2). In harkening back to that example of the endurance Jesus developed through His spiritual workouts, the writer of Hebrews speaks a similar word to us: "No discipline [or workout] seems pleasant at the time, but painful. Later on, however, it produces a harvest of righteousness and peace for those who have been trained by it" (Hebrews 12:11; see also Romans 5:3–5 and James 1:2–4).

Appropriate Rest

Athletes and trainers will often talk of their recovery regimens. Every workout session has to be followed by an appropriate time of rest and recovery—or in our wording, a time of sabbathing—or else we run the risk of over-exercise depleting us to the point where exercise becomes more harmful than helpful. Jesus understood this and listened to the Holy Spirit calling Him to a time of recovery. We see that "Jesus often withdrew to lonely places and prayed" after times of intense spiritual exercise (Luke 5:15–16).

When Jesus heard that King Herod had beheaded John the Baptist, He tried to "withdraw by boat privately to a solitary place," but crowds of people heard about this and followed Him. Jesus saw the desperate needs of this flock of sheep and "He had compassion on them." He healed them, He taught them, and He fed them (see Matthew 14:1–21). After this grueling day of spiritual exercise, notice how Jesus recovered:

Jesus made the disciples get into the boat and go on ahead of Him to the other side, while He dismissed the crowd. After He had dismissed them, He went up on a mountainside by Himself to pray. Later that night, He was there alone. (Matthew 14:22–23)

Jesus told us to get this same rest:

The apostles gathered around Jesus and reported to Him all they had done and taught. Then, because so many people were coming and going that they did not even have a chance to eat, He said to them, "Come with Me by yourselves to a quiet place and get some rest." So they went away by themselves in a boat to a solitary place. (Mark 6:30–32)

Evaluation and Adjustment

Both our physical and spiritual health practices will benefit from the wisdom of a wise coach. Our coach can point out areas that need changing: perhaps a tweak in our diet, a different exercise routine, or maybe a slight adjustment to our recovery times.

Within the Body of Christ, God has probably placed someone close to you who can give you some wise words from a fresh perspective. Have you noticed that the word "saints" in the New Testament is always in the plural, never the singular? That's because we need each other to bring out the saintly qualities in each other. This is why the writer of Hebrews stresses the camaraderie of "let us" so many times (Hebrews 10:22–25). I've found that many shepherd leaders tend to isolate. They are so involved in their own pasture of ministry that they seldom make the time to interact with other shepherds. In fact, isolation is one of the devil's favorite tactics. I encourage you to find friends—fellow saints—who are also committed to healthy spiritual growth and avail yourself of their friendship and insight.

As my friend Josh Schram reminded me, "Health is not just a big one-time choice. Health is small daily choices." Jesus made these daily choices to eat well, exercise regularly, rest when needed, and make the adjustments His Father spoke to His heart. He set us an example for healthy spiritual growth that will keep us in a place to grow our shepherding leadership capacities. Let's follow that example every single day.

12

THE PINNACLE OF
A SHEPHERD'S HEALTH

Everyone has a plan until
they get punched in the mouth.
—*Mike Tyson*

I was teaching a rather large adult Sunday school class as well as a Wednesday evening in-depth Bible study. Each class was roughly forty-five minutes long, and I worked hard to develop about forty-three minutes of high-quality content. I wanted to maximize every moment I had with these precious sheep by giving them the healthy spiritual food that would help them grow.

During this same period I had approached an older man in our church to ask him if he would mentor me, and he graciously agreed. Whenever we got together, Hank usually began with a penetrating question, so on one particular morning I was quite pleased when he asked,

"What have you been teaching in your classes?" I excitedly launched into a lengthy outline of the highly nutritious food I was preparing and serving.

Hank listened very attentively. When I finished, he smiled and asked, "And how are the folks living out what you're teaching?"

I was stumped, so I replied as honestly as I could, "I'm not sure I know how to answer that."

He smiled again while he waited for me to come up with another answer, but seeing that I was truly stumped, he simply said, "Have you asked them?"

The answer to that question was an emphatic "No." I was so focused on getting the teaching out that I never stopped to determine if it was indeed beneficial or even applicable to their lives. Back in my office later that afternoon, I made the decision to cut in half the amount of content I was trying to share and use the rest of our time together to hear people talk about how they may be able to use the material.

This was a risky move on my part. "What if," I mused, "they say something like, 'These lessons aren't applicable to my life'?" This, as it turned out, was pretty close to the truth. The following Sunday after I asked the class, "How do you think you could use this information this week?" I was greeted by silence. Uh oh!

So I went back to the drawing board. I started by going out to lunch with some of the people in the class and listening to what was happening in their lives. I heard about their successes and failures, their goals and fears, and their challenges and obstacles. Armed with this, I completely revamped all that I was teaching. I began to see people light up when I shared biblical insights that would truly help them where they lived and worked. This was a huge paradigm shift for me that has paid enormous benefits, but I never would have experienced this change without the loving prod from Hank.

There have been other changes I have made because of some not-so-loving prodding and poking. Hurting people hurt people, and I have been on the receiving end of those who are lashing out in pain. Sometimes people have criticized or insulted my leadership decisions. These have hurt. But what hurts me even more is when I look back on the immature ways I often responded in my younger days to those slights.

Getting to the Pinnacle

In chapter 8, I noted the unusual way Dr. Luke listed the healthy growth of our Chief Shepherd, with relational health being at the pinnacle. I think I would have expected spiritual health to be the highest health anyone can obtain. But think about this: How do I really know my spiritual health unless I am in close contact with others? I can say, "This is what I believe," but is that truly the way that I live? The sheep are watching us shepherds closely to see if we are "do-as-I-say" or "do-as-I-do" leaders.

The phrase Dr. Luke uses about Christ's growth is, "Jesus grew in favor with men." People liked having Jesus around. The word Luke uses for *favor* is from the same root word that is also translated "*grace*." Jesus was a graceful Man. Or we could say that He was a Man so full of grace that when He was jostled, only grace spilled out of Him.

What does it mean when someone is graceful? It means they are pleasant to be around. It means you feel safe around them, knowing they will never belittle you or put you down. It means that their focus is on your agenda, not their own agenda. It means they are a "there you are!" person, not a "here I am!" person. The bottom line: grace-full people are full of grace for others.

Jesus was healthy in His mind, His body, His spirit, and His emotions. This allowed Him to be in the place we noted earlier where He fully knew how powerful He was, yet He chose to use His power not for His own benefit, but to serve others (see John 13:1–4). Healthy love loves God and then serves God by loving and serving others. Only a wholly healthy person can truly serve with a right attitude. This is why relational health becomes the barometer of how healthy we are in the other areas.

People with a deficiency of wisdom don't serve because they don't know how to serve. People with unhealthy bodies can't serve because their disease has limited them. People with unhealthy spirits shouldn't serve because they would be serving with wrong motives, thus promoting hypocrisy. And people with unhealthy emotions won't serve because their superior attitude gets in the way. Only healthy shepherds can lead a flock of sheep to places where they too can be at their optimal health.

I have known some leaders that closet themselves away from their sheep, seldom interacting with them unless there is a "big issue" that demands their attention. I have also known others who are readily available when things are going well, but they disappear when someone is in need. One of the saddest things to see is when a shepherd is so run down mentally, physically, or spiritually that they simply cannot be present to meet the needs of their sheep.

We see nothing like this from Jesus. Remember that He operated on earth subjected to the same human limitations we all have. Jesus used His complete healthiness to serve: "For who is greater, the one who is at the table or the one who serves? Is it not the one who is at the table? *But I am among you as one who serves*" (Luke 22:27). The healthier the shepherd, the greater the impact the shepherd has on those he or she pastures.

Loving Reactions

We said earlier that an easy way to know if we have matured to a servant-hearted shepherd leader is when we don't mind being treated as a servant. But the question is: How do we know this is the attitude that we actually have?

Let's return to our perfect example in Jesus. He was treated rudely and spoken to condescendingly, even by people who should have been His allies. Then there were those on a constant mission to try to trip Him up or get Him to say or do something that would have undermined His credibility. Yet Jesus never spoke inappropriately nor acted childishly. Jesus never had to say, "My bad, I misspoke there," or "Sorry, I shouldn't have done that."

We can make all of our plans to behave in loving ways toward the sheep under our care, but what happens when the sheep ignore us, bite us, or leave us? As boxer Mike Tyson noted, "Everyone has a plan until they get punched in the mouth." Surely the best indication of our overall healthiness and servant-like attitude is not so much our actions but our reactions. The way I react may say more about my health as a leader than the way I act or plan to act.

Was Jesus ever punched in the mouth? Not only figuratively, but literally He was! But Peter noted, "When they hurled their insults at [Jesus], He did not retaliate; when He suffered, He made no threats" (1 Peter 2:23). There were some people that Jesus chose to engage in conversation, and there were others from whom He walked away. There were some people He went of out His way to see, and others who interrupted His journey or His teaching with their urgent requests. Whatever the setting and whoever the audience, Jesus never misspoke nor misacted, no matter how rudely He was treated.

David had decided on an effective strategy when he was around people who had a tendency to push his buttons: "I will put a muzzle on my mouth while in the presence of the wicked" (Psalm 39:1). Have you made a decision like that before? Have you ever had an inappropriate word still slip out, despite your vow to keep it in? That so-called "slip of the tongue" is actually a blessing, because it reveals what is really in your heart (see Matthew 15:19). You might try to excuse it by saying, "I was caught off guard," but C.S. Lewis reminds us that justification just won't fly:

> When I come to my evening prayers and try to reckon up the sins of the day, nine times out of ten the most obvious one is some sin against charity; I have sulked or snapped or sneered or snubbed or stormed. And the excuse that immediately springs to mind is that the provocation was so sudden or unexpected. I was caught off my guard, I had not time to collect myself.... Surely what a man does when he is taken off guard is the best evidence of

what sort of man he is. Surely what pops out before the man has time to put on a disguise is the truth. If there are rats in the cellar you are most likely to see them if you go in very suddenly. But the suddenness did not create the rats; it only prevents them from hiding. In the same way, the suddenness of the provocation does not make me an ill-tempered man: it only shows what an ill-tempered man I am.

So what did our reaction just reveal? There are some rats that are still lurking in our hearts. Nothing builds more leadership credibility among a flock of sheep, and nothing builds a more God-centered heart in a shepherd than the shepherd saying, "I was wrong. I misspoke. I acted inappropriately. Please forgive me. I'm going to allow the Holy Spirit to help me clean up that area so that never happens again." Shepherds need to be among their sheep, leading, teaching, getting jostled, getting bit, getting interrupted, getting mistreated, and then be able to prayerfully evaluate their loving or unloving reactions.

Christlike reactions are the pinnacle of a shepherd's health.

When your reactions aren't Christlike, admit it. Someone might want to push back, "But if I say I was wrong, then I may lose some leadership credibility." I would agree that you will lose credibility *if* you believe you are a self-made leader and *if* you are climbing up a career ladder that you designed. But if you are truly living and leading as a servant that God has equipped and placed among this flock, admission of an un-Christlike action or reaction triggers something extraordinary: God's help. Peter said it this way: "All of you, clothe yourselves with humility toward one another, because, 'God opposes the proud but shows favor to the humble'" (1 Peter 5:5).

Did you catch that? God stands back from the proud person who will not admit his error nor ask for help, let alone ask for forgiveness. On the other hand, God lavishes His grace on the humble one who admits both his error and his need for help. Admission of an inappropriate action or reaction brings God's help!

Friends, the mark of a maturing shepherd is not one who never misspeaks or never makes a mistake. No, the mark of a maturing shepherd is the one who is closing the gap between his mess up and his confession, and one who is experiencing fewer mess ups over time because the Holy Spirit is helping him get healthier and more mature.

The pinnacle of a shepherd leader's health is not how wise you are, nor how physically healthy, nor even how much spiritual insight you have gained, but it is how appropriately God-honoring your actions and reactions are among the sheep you pasture.

If you see or hear something from yourself that is not reflective of your Chief Shepherd, it's how you handle your next response that reveals how close you are getting to the pinnacle of health that Jesus demonstrated for you.

13

GOING FARTHER

If you want to go fast, go alone.
If you want to go far, go together.
—Kenyan Proverb

Samuel Cooper was laboring over an official portrait of Oliver Cromwell. General Cromwell had a couple of warts on his face, and Cooper thought he would do a great service to the legacy of Cromwell if he omitted the disfiguring warts. When the portrait was unveiled for Cromwell, he looked at for a moment and said, "Take it away, and paint me warts and all."

I'm glad that the Holy Spirit inspired the biblical writers to give us the accounts of the lives of key historical figures with all of their assets and liabilities on full display—we get to see them "warts and all." I find comfort in knowing that God uses flawed people as His shepherd leaders. In looking at these wart accounts, I see an important warning for today's shepherd leaders.

David was the gold standard for every king of Israel who followed him. Numerous times throughout the history of Israel, we will see a note that a certain king either followed God like David, or turned from God unlike David. Yet there exists a wart on David's portrait: an adulteress affair with the wife of a man in his inner circle, and then subsequent lies and a murder to cover up the affair. "The thing David had done displeased the Lord" (see 2 Samuel 11).

But I'd like to turn your attention to when this affair occurred: "In the spring, at the time when kings go off to war ... David remained in Jerusalem" (2 Samuel 11:1). He was without his usual comrades. The men who knew David best, who could probably sense if something was amiss, weren't around to warn him. When David tried to find out the identity of the bathing beauty on the roof next door to his palace, an unnamed attendant tried to remind him, "Isn't that Bathsheba, the *wife* of Uriah?" but David dismissed him.

Elijah was arguably the most forceful and fearless prophet in Israel's history. Not only did he stand up to the evil kings of Israel, but he spoke out against the kings of surrounding nations, too. In answer to Elijah's prayer, God brought a drought on the land, and again in answer to Elijah's prayer, God sent rain. Elijah challenged the 450 prophets of the god Baal and the 400 prophets of the goddess Asherah to a duel to the death, which ended up in a decisive victory for Yahweh. Yet, shortly after this massive victory, Elijah was depressed to the point that he wanted to die.

What led to Elijah's depression? Something very similar to David's slide into adultery: He was alone. Elijah ran away from Queen Jezebel's death threat, left his servant behind, and proceeded all by himself into the desert. It was when he was without a comrade that he prayed to God, "I've had enough. Take my life" (see 2 Kings 17–19).

And what about Peter? He boldly claimed his loyalty to Jesus, even to the point of wielding a sword at the guards who came to arrest his Master. But when Peter was alone, after the other disciples fled, he denied three times that he knew Jesus (Matthew 26:33, 51, 69–75).

God designed us to be in relationship with others. His statement to Adam in some of the earliest words of the Bible—"It is not good for you to be alone"—are words for us still today. As I mentioned earlier, you will not find the word "saints" in the singular in the New Testament. Instead, you will find such phrases as "one another," "each other," and "all together" prominently displayed throughout the New Testament church. Let me say it again: God designed us to be in relationship with others. If you want to go far in your shepherding, you cannot try to go alone.

Prayer for More Shepherds

Notice that Jesus sent His disciples out in twos. The early church followed His example, so we never see anyone being sent on ministry assignments by themselves. As Solomon reminded us:

> *Two are better than one, because they have a good return for their labor: If either of them falls down, one can help the other up. But pity anyone who falls and has no one to help them up. Also, if two lie down together, they will keep warm. But how can one keep warm alone? Though one may be overpowered, two can defend themselves. A cord of three strands is not quickly broken.* (Ecclesiastes 4:9–12)

You will not only extend your leadership by having other servant-hearted shepherds around you, but you will also have a guard against the aloneness that led to such ugly warts on the biography of otherwise powerful leaders such as David, Elijah, and Peter.

Jesus told us to pray to the Lord of the Harvest to send out more workers into the field (Luke 10:2). In a similar attitude, I believe we can pray to the Chief Shepherd to send out more under-shepherds into the pastures; specifically, we can pray for those under-shepherds to be sent into the pasture where we labor. The early church showed us the example of prayer being the priority when new shepherds were needed (Acts 1:21–26, 6:3–6, 13:1–3; 2 Timothy 1:3–6). We would do well to make it a priority to pray for God to send us godly leaders that can serve alongside us.

Raising Up More Shepherds

The first step to raising up more leaders is to maintain that healthy balance between confidence and humility. Overly confident leaders can send a signal to others that their partnership is unnecessary, and overly humble leaders will have a difficult time casting a compelling, exciting vision for their organization. But a leader that is striving to stay humbly confident or confidently humble can attract potential shepherds by a compelling vision in which the emerging leader feels he can play a vital role in fulfilling.

A properly balanced leader also recognizes that his leadership is vital but not exclusive. In Ephesians 4, Paul talks about the gifts God has given to equip the people. These gifts are called apostles, prophets, evangelists, shepherds, and teachers. Notice that these are gifts, not titles. These gifts, like all gifts or talents God gives or investments that God makes, are intended to have a return on investment. In this case, God is looking for unity and maturity that result in healthy sheep reproducing more healthy sheep.

Years ago, President Dwight Eisenhower said, "Never let yourself be persuaded that one Great Man, and one leader, is necessary to the salvation of America. When America consists of one leader and 158 million followers, it will no longer be America." We could correctly paraphrase his quote this way, "Never let yourself be persuaded that you are the one great leader that is solely necessary for the success of the flock under your care. When you believe you are *the* leader and everyone else follows you, you will no longer be leading a healthy organization."

If you are a shepherd, it is not your role to do all of the work. Your primarily job is to create a healthy environment for the sheep to flourish. When you do this, healthy sheep will reproduce. If you are a pastor of a church, it is not your role to do all of the ministry, but to equip others to minister. If you run a nonprofit organization, it is not your role to handle every single detail, but to allow others to use the gifts that God has implanted in them. What a huge burden this takes off shepherds when they realize that they don't have to oversee every single detail.

But let's be careful not to go to the other extreme. I've met far too many leaders who lock themselves away from others. They mistakenly feel that they need to maintain a buffer between themselves and their constituents or teammates. But how can a shepherd guide his or her sheep from a distance?

Jesus said not only that He knew His sheep, but that His sheep knew Him, too. Shepherd leaders get right into the messiness of shepherding. Let's be honest: pastures are not very neat, tidy places to hang out. But pastures are where the sheep are, so that is where the shepherds need to be. If the only time you interact with others is when you want to make an announcement or someone needs to be corrected, your sheep will begin to either resent you or fear your arrival.

Every person has a unique personality. God has never duplicated a single person. Ever! So the people around you are one-of-a-kind creations, and as their shepherd, it is your delightful responsibility to get to know them personally and individually. Discover the gifts of all the sheep, their talents, their quirkiness, their dreams, and their fears. Be available to laugh and cry with them, to teach them, and to learn from them. In doing this, you will begin to discover new under-shepherds who can come alongside you, extending your leadership reach.

Our churches, parachurches, and nonprofit organizations should be among the safest places in the world for emerging shepherds to experiment, stretch, and grow. Will it be painful at times? It sure will! But the joy of helping an emerging leader find the place where God has uniquely equipped him to minister is beyond compare to the inevitable painful moments caused by immature leaders who are eager to minister.

Consider an emerging leader named John Mark. He was asked to join the missionary team of Barnabas and Saul. Barnabas initially took the lead role on this trip, but as Saul matured in his abilities, he not only changed his name to Paul to signify this new Christian maturity, but Barnabas also stepped aside to let Paul take the lead role. This apparently was a difficult transition for Mark, and he soon left the team to return to Jerusalem. Mark's departure was obviously very painful and disappointing to Paul. We can tell this because some time later, when Paul and Barnabas were going to make a follow-up journey, Barnabas suggested they give Mark a second chance, and Paul flatly refused. He claimed Mark had deserted them, and he wasn't willing to open himself up to that disappointment again. As a result, Barnabas and Paul parted company, with Barnabas taking Mark with him, and Paul taking Silas (see Acts 13:4, 13; 15:36–40).

That may have been the end of the story for Mark. But Barnabas believed in him and continued to invest in him. Although Luke's historical account doesn't follow the missionary journey of Barnabas and Mark, nor does he give us any insight into the training Mark received from Barnabas, Paul gives us the clearest indication of the growth in maturity of Mark. Sitting alone in a Roman prison, facing an imminent execution, Paul wrote to Timothy how abandoned he felt by other teammates. Paul asked Timothy to bring him a coat and some manuscripts to read, and then he added these amazing words: "Get Mark and bring him with you, because he is helpful to me in my ministry" (2 Timothy 4:11).

What a testament to Barnabas who not only saw the value in Saul/Paul and put his reputation on the line for him, but who also wouldn't give up on an immature Mark. Barnabas kept investing in him so that he was called helpful by the man who formerly called him a deserter. That's why shepherds must continue to stay close to their sheep to identify those who may be emerging shepherds. They may be immature or hot-headed or unsure or timid or even one-time deserters. But we continue to invest in them, believing in the worth God has implanted in them, and seeking a return on investment that will take our leadership capacity further than we could have taken it on our own.

If you want to go far, don't try to go alone. If you want an accountability partner that can keep warts away from your leadership legacy, don't go alone. If you want to extend your leadership influence, don't go alone. If you want to honor God's investment in you, don't go alone.

14

DON'T TRY TO GROW
YOUR MINISTRY

Success, success to you, and success
to those who help you,
for your God will help you.
—Amasai, the leader of King David's Mighty Men
(1 Chronicles 12:18)

Back in the first chapter I wrote, "God's ladder of success is nothing like ours." Indeed, a quick search of the word "success" in the Bible reveals very little that looks like the metrics we typically associate with the word today.

The Bible shows us that success could be attentively serving the master God has placed over us (see the examples of Abraham's servant in Genesis 24, and Nehemiah and Daniel as they served under foreign kings), or doing our work in a way that acknowledges and honors God (Deuteronomy 16:15). But without a close second, the predominant way the Scriptures define success is obeying God (just a handful of examples include Genesis 39:3, 23; Joshua 1:8; 1 Samuel 18:14, 30; John 3:29). Interestingly, the word "success" is virtually non-existent in the New Testament, so that means we must be very cautious in our definitions of what we think success is.

Not on the Same Page

I was called in to facilitate a conversation between the board and staff of a nonprofit organization. The mission statement sounded compelling, and already the organization had some great buy-in from key community leaders. And yet, the organization was struggling to find its way.

I began my time with them by passing around stacks of Post-It notes to every member of the board and staff. I asked them to write down answers to several questions including:

- What's the biggest need in our community that our organization can address?
- What is our unique strength?
- What is standing in the way of us being successful?

As the participants began to fill up these notes, we stuck them all over the walls in the conference room where we were meeting. After everyone had finished writing, I called for a ten-minute coffee break. While they were socializing with one another, I began to group the Post-It notes together in clusters of similar thought. Soon there emerged several collages of brightly-colored squares in about five or six different categories.

As the participants returned from their break, I began by asking some clarifying questions about one particular category. This cluster was by far the largest, and since all of the participants had been working independently, it seemed to be a good bet that they all had this one area at the forefront of their minds. As I was asking some more specific questions, I began to feel a tension in the room—people were shifting in their seats, and there was a definite agitation building up—but still I persisted with my questions.

Finally, one board member spoke up: "Why are you spending so much time on this?"

"Do you think this isn't an important topic?" I pushed back. "This is the largest cluster from your own responses, so it appears to be important to everyone here."

"Well," he said, "we know how to handle this one."

"Oh," I responded, as though I was surprised, "how would you address this?"

"Our board will just raise more money," he said flatly.

I paused to see if anyone else would weigh in. I noticed that the board members were all nodding in agreement, but the staff members sat expressionless. So I called on the director: "What about that? Do you think more money will address this concern? Do you think you can spend your way to success?"

The director swallowed hard before barely whispering, "No."

This is a common disconnect in nonprofit organizations and churches. Many of the boards of these organizations are wonderful, godly people who fully believe in the mission of the organization. These board members are often successful business people who have both wisdom and wealth to contribute to the organization. But here's the problem: the way we define success in a for-profit organization isn't the same way we define success in a nonprofit organization. And often the way we define success in any of our ministries doesn't line up with the Bible's definition.

Business people are accustomed to making a financial investment in their business and then see a return on their investment that is readily apparent on the bottom line of the financial report. Shepherd leaders shouldn't measure success like a CEO, looking at the bottom line. They should measure success like a shepherd: concerned solely with how healthy the environment is for their sheep. CEOs have to give an account to shareholders on the profit that has been made. Shepherd leaders have to give an account to the Chief Shepherd of how well they have leveraged the talents that have been given them.

I was talking to the board of a pregnancy resource center (PRC). I noted that if they invested $10,000 in their own businesses, perhaps they would be looking at a profit of something like $25,000 by the end of their fiscal year. But if $10,000 were given to this PRC, they were going to spend every single cent of it; there would be no financial profit to show at the end of the year. However, the PRC could point to something else: they could show how many abortion-minded women had changed their minds and didn't abort their babies. How do you put a price tag on a saved life?

Businesses think in terms of quantitative gains—things they can count—but churches and nonprofits should be thinking in terms of qualitative gains—a quality improvement that isn't as easily counted. I think we all know this, and yet we still persist in wanting to define success in a church or a nonprofit by those quantitative standards such as attendance growth, donations, and the like. When we think qualitative over quantitative, suddenly what seemed "small" is so significant and so valuable that it cannot be calculated! What if one of those babies that wasn't aborted discovers a cure for cancer, or deciphers a dialect to take the Gospel to an unreached people group, or becomes the loving next-door neighbor that leads your son or daughter to a relationship with Jesus?

The Value of the Sheep

Just as you cannot put a price tag on a life, you cannot put a price tag on a sheep. Make no mistake about it, God views His sheep—every single one of them—as invaluable. Because His valuation is so high, we can understand why He gets so angry at those who are more concerned about their success than they are about the health of the sheep. When God uses the word "Woe!" we should definitely take that seriously. He uses that very word to warn shepherd leaders who were shirking their responsibility when He said, "Woe to those shepherds who only take care of themselves" (Ezekiel 34:2).

When we map out *our* plan for success, or when we try to define success solely by quantitative measurements, we ultimately become more committed to our plans than to God's sheep. God pulls no punches when He calls leaders with this attitude evil, mere hired hands, or even thieves (Jeremiah 23:3; John 10:8, 12). And most sobering of all, God says, "I will hold them accountable" (Ezekiel 34:10).

Oswald Chambers has a poignant question for us: "When we stand before God, will He say, 'Well done, good and faithful servant'? or will He say, 'You have not been a shepherd of My sheep, you have fed them for your own interest, exploited them for your own creed'?"

Shepherd leaders do need to work on themselves. They need to add humility to their confidence and confidence to their humility, they need to cultivate stick-to-it-iveness, they need to be wholly healthy, and they need to raise up more shepherd leaders to assist them. But woe to the shepherds who do these things only so they can say, "Look at how successful I have become!" The God-pleasing attitude that every shepherd leader needs to be sure is in place is the one that says, "I have only obediently served God by caring for His sheep." Jesus said it this way:

Will [the master] thank the servant because he did what he was told to do? So you also, when you have done everything you were told to do, should say, "We are unworthy servants; we have only done our duty." (Luke 17:9–10)

Every sheep is invaluable. God knows where to place or remove shepherds to care for His sheep. Just as we can review the pages of history to see when and where God raised up world leaders to fulfill His plan, He is still doing that today to fulfill the plan for each and every sheep that is so dear to Him.

Don't Do It Yourself

Don't try to grow your ministry. First, because it's not *yours*, it's His; and second, because your measure of success is probably more slanted toward quantitative measurements than qualitative. Jesus wasn't concerned about bigger numbers: "What do you think?" He asked, "If a man has a hundred sheep, and one of them goes astray, does he not leave the ninety-nine and go to the mountains to seek the one that is straying?" (Matthew 18:12).

Philip went to Samaria to tell people about Jesus. He didn't go there because it fit his plan, but because Jesus said, "You will be My witnesses in Jerusalem, and in all Judea and Samaria, and to the ends of the earth" (Acts 1:8). Philip's obedience brought God's success: hundreds turned to Jesus as their Savior, demon-possessed people were delivered, the sick were healed, and the new Christians were baptized in the Holy Spirit. Yet God called Philip to leave these "ninety-nine" and go to the desert to cross paths with just one confused and wondering sheep (Acts 8). After that, Philip virtually disappears from Luke's historical record.

What's the value of one government official's life? God says that his value is incalculable. Apparently, God knew that Philip was the perfect shepherd to lead this Ethiopian to the pasture where he would accept Jesus as his Savior. Philip was obedient, a sheep was saved, and God was pleased. But I wonder how many people today might think Philip's ministry was unsuccessful because he left a bigger ministry in Samaria to go to a smaller ministry in the desert? Bishop William C. Abney said, "I'm still waiting for a leader to say, 'God called me to a smaller ministry.' We usually only say, 'God called me' when it's something bigger. God's math doesn't work our way."

The Chief Shepherd made this commitment to His sheep: "And I will give you shepherds according to My heart, who will feed you with knowledge and understanding" (Jeremiah 3:15). My prayer is that we would much rather feed a few sheep where God has directed us and given us His heart than for us to try to manufacture success that is measured by how many nickels and noses we can count.

15

APPLAUSE

Self-promotion is an anti-God attitude.

—*Craig T. Owens*

In the midst of the shutdowns during the coronavirus craziness, I was attempting to stay in touch with pastors in my community and to be an encouragement to them. I said to one pastor, "I'm not asking about your flock, but I'm asking about you: How are *you* doing?"

"Well," he responded dejectedly, "I'm just trying to adjust to the new metrics."

"New metrics," I repeated. "What do you mean?"

"When we were meeting in person, there would be upwards of 250 in attendance, but now that we're only broadcasting our Sunday morning service online, we are only having about 30 tune in. Does that mean that only 30 people really care?"

We seem to be fixated on numbers.

Long before there were any shutdowns, pastor friends would ask me, "How are things going?"

I would always respond, "Fantastic!"

Almost without fail, their very next question would be, "How many are you running on Sundays?"

"What if I said 300?" I'd ask. At this their smile would usually widen, but then I would quickly add, "What if I said 20?" And their smile usually changed to confusion.

"Here's the real question," I would say. "How many lives are being transformed? How many of those transformed people are actively and daily living out their Christian testimony? Wouldn't it be far better to have 20 world-changers than 300 that only attend church on Sunday morning?"

I've heard all the clichés: "Well, there's a book in the Bible called Numbers, so obviously God is interested in numerical growth." But those folks also conveniently leave out God's anger at David for counting his fighting men, or that Jesus said, "Small is the gate and narrow the road that leads to life, and only a few find it" (Matthew 7:14). Don't get me wrong: God desires that none should perish, but He doesn't gauge a shepherd's success solely on numbers but on the shepherd's faithfulness.

What Success Is and Isn't

"We need a plan to grow the church," one of the board members said to me.

"What do you mean by 'grow'?" I asked.

"You know, *grow* the church," he said with a little more emphasis, as if that would define the word.

I reminded him that just repeating the word didn't define it any more clearly. I sat there looking at all of the board members, and they looked back at me. I could tell that they thought I was pretty dense for not understanding the word "grow," so I offered a solution.

"Your church is on a main road with a pretty high traffic volume, and you've got a nice marquis sign out front." They all nodded in agreement. "So," I continued, "let's change the message on the sign to read: 'Free $50 gift certificate for all first-time visitors.' That should pack the church on Sunday morning!"

They continued to stare at me as though I were speaking a foreign language, so I asked, "Is that not what you meant by 'grow'?"

Growth and success may need to be redefined in your church or ministry. If you've been thinking that success is a steadily upward climb in attendance or donations, or a bigger facility, or more people on staff, then it would appear that the ministries of Philip, Paul, and even Jesus were highly unsuccessful. We've already seen that Philip went from a large revival in Samaria to one person in the desert. Paul came to the end of his life telling Timothy how many of his companions had abandoned him. And Jesus started His public ministry with twelve emerging leaders, only to see one betray Him, nine run away when He was arrested, and one deny that he even knew Him.

When we come up with our plans to "grow" our ministry, or we say "success" is all about what we can count, aren't we really just self-promoting? As we saw in the words of Peter in the previous chapter, self-promotion is an anti-God attitude. Self-promotion proudly says, "God, here are *my* plans that I want You to bless."

When we try to imitate what someone else has done that has apparently brought numeric success, are we really trusting God, or are we simply copying another shepherd? Paul and Peter and Apollos were confronting this wrong thinking at the outset of the New Testament church:

> *When one of you says, "I am a follower of Paul," and another says, "I follow Apollos," aren't you acting just like people of the world? After all, who is Apollos? Who is Paul? We are only God's servants through whom you believed the Good News. Each of us did the work the Lord gave us. I planted the seed in your hearts, and Apollos watered it, but it was God who made it grow. It's not important who does the planting, or who does the watering. What's important is that God makes the seed grow. The one who plants and the one who waters work together with the*

same purpose. And both will be rewarded for their own hard work. (1 Corinthians 3:4–8 NLT)

Did you catch that? Twice Paul reminds us that it is God who makes things grow. God, not man. So is the only successful ministry the one that harvests? How did they harvest without someone watering the seed? What exactly were they watering if no one had planted any seeds? And even with everyone doing the work, it is still God who makes things grow.

According to Paul, what does God reward? It's not numeric growth, but shepherds "will be rewarded for their own hard work ... the work the Lord gave us."

God stands off from those who proudly concoct their own plans for success. God cannot use those who are too fearful to trust Him. But God gives grace—His limitless help—to those who are confidently humble or humbly confident in working hard to serve God's sheep right where God has placed them. Then Jesus promises, "The greatest among you will be your servant" (Matthew 23:11).

Applause

If God has called you to be a shepherd leader, then lead with the full assurance that He will never let you down nor fail to supply all that you need to lead well. Leading in this God-honoring way is leading successfully.

Joshua had been through years of extensive preparation to become Moses' successor. He was a recognized leader in his tribe, the general of the army, and a personal assistant to Moses. But his most important leadership qualification was this: He was called by God to shepherd the sheep of Israel after Moses' death. Joshua could say with humble confidence, "God chose me."

As the story of Joshua's leadership opens in the first chapter of the book of the Bible named for him, God gives four requirements for Joshua to be effective in his leadership role. This is still relevant for shepherd leaders today.

First, be yourself. God didn't say, "Be like Moses." In fact, the only time God talks about Moses to Joshua is to reassure him: "I will be with you as I was with Moses." But never once does God use a "Moses Grading Scale" for Joshua. God simply says, "*You* will lead these people."

Second, Joshua needed to have an objective measuring stick. Feelings may change, but God's Word never does. So God counsels Joshua to always rely on the Book of the Law.

Third, Joshua was challenged to guard his thoughts. Shepherds can have so many sheep "in their ear" baaing as they lobby for what they want. So God tells Joshua to not only read the Bible but also to continually meditate on it. One definition of meditation is to *hum* God's Word.

In other words, humming God's Word will help a leader know which sheep's voice is in harmony with God's voice, and which voice is off-key.

Finally, Joshua needed to guard his attitude. God repeats this to Joshua: "Do not be afraid; do not be discouraged." Even when doing everything they are supposed to be doing, leaders can become afraid to make a change, or they may become discouraged because people aren't following along. These feelings must be driven out with one firm declaration: "God chose me. I know He has called me to this leadership position, so I know He is with me. He will enable me to complete what He has called me to do."

In Matthew 25, Jesus tells us quite a bit about success in the Chief Shepherd's eyes, and not one of the measurements of success has anything to do with numeric or financial growth, the size of a church building, or the number of people being served by a particular ministry. Jesus said that it was about people who saw hurting individuals and ministered to them.

Shepherd leaders feed hungry sheep, and they get water to the thirsty and clothes to the naked. Shepherds make sure that the imprisoned are visited and that no one is left alone. To those who faithfully pasture this way, the Master says, "Well done, good and faithful servant."

Servant. Think about that word. The faithful servant is the one who does whatever is needed for his master and for those his master cares about. The faithful servant doesn't work solely for a paycheck. The faithful servant doesn't count how many people he has waited on or how many thank-you notes he has received.

As I said before, sheep are often ungrateful. You are more likely to hear from sheep who are upset than from those who are grateful. And, sadly, many of the sheep who do express a form of gratitude are doing so only as a way to flatter you and try to gain influence with you. Those flatterers will usually abandon you as soon as they get "a better offer" from another shepherd.

My friend, the only applause that you should care about is from nail-scarred hands. The only words and the only recognition that matter for all of eternity come from the Chief Shepherd who says, "Well done, good and faithful servant."

Heavenly Father, I pray for my fellow shepherds. The work You have called them to is hard, unrelenting, draining, and often thankless. The enemy of Your sheep is looking for an opening to pounce. He wants to steal, kill, and destroy Your sheep, and often he will start with the shepherd. He knows Your word that says, "Strike the shepherd, and the sheep of the flock will be scattered" (Matthew 26:31).

So I pray that You would remind Your shepherds that You called them. Let this simple phrase add confidence to their humility and humility to their confidence. Keep them from the human desire to make their plans, or to be distracted by a measure of success that isn't biblical or honoring of You. Help them to make the changes that are necessary to be wholly healthy leaders so that they can bring health and wholeness to Your flock under their care. And above all, I pray that You would help their ears to silence all other cheers and jeers as they listen only for applause from Your nail-scarred hands. May all of us together lead and shepherd in a way that honors You and earns the ultimate reward as You say to us, "Well done, My good and faithful servant."

In Jesus' name I pray this for my friends. Amen!

ACKNOWLEDGMENTS

My parents and my wife would frequently ask me, "When are you going to write a book?"

I always gave them the same answer: "I wouldn't even know the first step in the process."

I am grateful to my parents, Ray and Claudia, and my wife Betsy for believing I had it in me to write a book before even I could see it myself.

Betsy, you are my very best friend! No one on earth has—or continues to have—such an influence on me like you do. You continue to be such a source of inspiration.

Then along came Tom Freiling. Although he and Betsy and I all attended Oral Roberts University at the same time, God kept us from crossing paths then. It was only recently that God allowed Tom to stumble across my blog. After poking around there, Tom emailed to say, "Have you ever thought about writing a book?" and I gave him the same answer I gave my parents and my wife. But Tom knew not only the first step in the process, but all of the steps to completion. Thanks, Tom, for guiding this project.

I had some ideas, but getting them down in a way that made sense was another matter. Enter Christen Jeschke. She studiously read every chapter and offered the insightful critiques that helped this book come together better than I had even imagined.

The writer of Proverbs says that like iron sharpening iron, a friend can sharpen our lives. I'm so blessed to have such an iron-sharp friend in Greg Heeres. Greg is the other half of *The Craig and Greg Show* leadership podcast, but he is so much more than that. For over thirty years, he has been my covenant brother. Greg, thank you for your encouragement, your wisdom, and your friendship. Your investment in me has paid dividends in the way I've been able to invest in others.

My kids keep me grounded. They are my joy as I watch them stretch their wings and soar. Harrison, Tabi, Samantha, Ian, and Brandon, you will never know how much I treasure you.

Finally, I have to give a huge shout-out to my family at Calvary Assembly of God! You all bless me in the way you grow in your love for Jesus and the way you want to make Him seen in our community. I ♥ my church!

ABOUT THE AUTHOR

Craig T. Owens has been blessed to work in a variety of leadership positions, in both the for-profit and non-profit worlds. He pastors Calvary Assembly of God, co-hosts a leadership podcast called *The Craig and Greg Show*, is a frequent consultant to leaders in other organizations, and authors a highly trafficked blog and a popular daily podcast.

Craig has been married to Betsy, his first girlfriend, since 1990, and they have three children and an amazing daughter-in-love and son-in-love. They live and pasture in Cedar Springs, Michigan.

Craig's passion is to see biblical principles lived out in the daily lives of Christians, so all of his writings, and sermons, and consultations are steeped in Scripture. Keep up with Craig's daily thoughts on his blog at http://craigtowens.com. You can also follow Craig on Twitter @craigtowens or on his Facebook page @craigtowensblog. And be sure to check out the Craig T. Owens Audio Blog on Spotify, Apple, or Audible.